The
Supporters'
Guide
to
Non-League
Football
1998

EDITOR
John Robinson

Sixth Edition

CONTENTS

British Library Cataloguing in Publication Data

A catalogue record for this book is available from the British Library

ISBN 1-86223-002-1

Copyright © 1997; SOCCER BOOKS LIMITED (01472-696226)

72, St. Peters' Avenue, Cleethorpes, N.E. Lincolnshire, DN35 8HU, England

Printed by Adlard Print & Typesetting Services, The Old School, The Green, Ruddington, Notts. NG11 6HH

FOREWORD

Our thanks go to the numerous club officials who have aided us in the compilation of the information contained in this guide and also to Michael Robinson (page layouts) and Ceri Sampson (cover artwork) for the part they have played. We are also indebted to the secretaries of the various leagues for providing statistical information and extensive support.

Although we use the term 'Child' for concessionary prices, this is usually the price charged to Senior Citizens also. We welcome comments from readers as to items which they feel should be included in future editions.

Finally, we would like to wish our readers a happy and safe spectating season.

John Robinson

EDITOR

CHELTENHAM TOWN FC

Founded: 1892
Former Name(s): None
Nickname: 'Robins'
Ground: Whaddon Road, Cheltenham,
Gloucestershire GL52 5NA
Record Attendance: 8,326 (1956)
Social Club Phone No.: (01242) 521974

Colours: Shirts - Red, White & Black
Shorts - Black
Telephone No.: (01242) 573558 (Office)
Daytime Phone: (01242) 513397 (Secretary)
Pitch Size: 110 × 73yds
Ground Capacity: 6,000
Seating Capacity: 1,200

GENERAL INFORMATION
Supporters Club Administrator:
John Regan, Robins Benefit Committee
Address: c/o Club
Telephone Number: (01242) 573558
Car Parking: At Ground (120 spaces)
Coach Parking: Wymans Road
Nearest Railway Station: Cheltenham Spa
(2 miles)
Nearest Bus Station: Cheltenham Royal Well
Club Shop: Yes
Opening Times: Matchdays Only & Office
during week
Telephone No.: (01242) 573558
Postal Sales: Yes
Nearest Police Station: Whaddon,
Cheltenham
Police Force: Gloucestershire
Police Telephone No.: (01242) 528282

GROUND INFORMATION
Away Supporters' Entrances: Wymans Road Side
Away Supporters' Sections: (Only certain matches)

DISABLED INFORMATION
Wheelchairs: Accommodated around ground
Disabled Toilets: None
Contact Nº: (01242) 573558

ADMISSION INFO (1997/98 PRICES)
Adult Standing: £6.00
Adult Seating: £7.00
Child Standing: £2.00
Child Seating: £3.00
Concessionary Standing: £4.00
Concessionary Seating: £5.00
Programme Price: £1.00
FAX Number: (01242) 224675

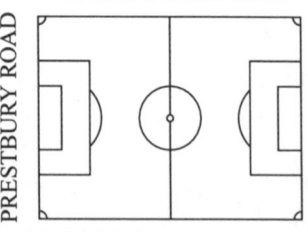

Travelling Supporters Information:
Routes: The Ground is situated to the North-East of Cheltenham, 1 mile from the Town Centre off the
B4632 (Prestbury Road) – Whaddon Road is to the East of the B4632 just North of Pittville Circus. Road
signs in the vicinity indicate 'Whaddon Road/ Cheltenham Town FC'.

DOVER ATHLETIC FC

Founded: 1983
Former Name(s): None
Nickname: 'Lilywhites'
Ground: Crabble Athletic Ground, Lewisham Road, River, Dover, Kent
Record Attendance: 4,035 vs Bromsgrove Rovers (1992)

Colours: Shirts - White
Shorts - Black
Telephone No.: (01304) 822373
Daytime Phone No.: (01304) 240041
Pitch Size: 110 × 75yds
Ground Capacity: 6,500
Seating Capacity: 1,000

GENERAL INFORMATION
Supporters Club Administrator:
Chris Graves
Address: Dover Athletic Supporters Club, 4 Albert Road, Canterbury, Kent CT1 1UJ
Telephone Number: (01227) 769708
Car Parking: Street Parking
Coach Parking: Street Parking
Nearest Railway Station: Kearsney (1 mile)
Nearest Bus Station: Pencester Road, Dover (1.5 miles)
Club Shop: At ground and 15 Worthington Street, Dover
Opening Times: Matchdays at ground and Monday to Friday at the other shop
Telephone No.: (01304) 240041
Postal Sales: Yes
Nearest Police Station: Dover
Police Force: Kent County Constabulary
Police Telephone No.: (01304) 240055

GROUND INFORMATION
Away Supporters' Entrances: No Segregation
Away Supporters' Sections: -

DISABLED INFORMATION
Wheelchairs: Approximately 20 spaces available in total in front of the Family Stand
Disabled Toilets: None
Contact Nº: (01227) 769708

ADMISSION INFO (1997/98 PRICES)
Adult Standing: £6.50
Adult Seating: £7.50
Child Standing: £3.50   (Under 12's £1.00)
Child Seating: £4.00
Programme Price: £1.20
FAX Number: (01304) 210273

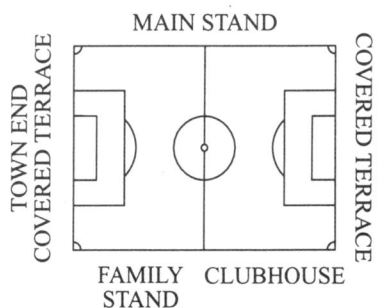

Travelling Supporters Information:
Routes: By A2 to Whitfield roundabout. Take 4th exit down hill to mini-roundabout – turn left – go 1 mile to traffic lights on hill. Turn sharp right, under railway bridge – ground is on left a further 300 yards.

FARNBOROUGH TOWN FC

Founded: 1967	**Colours**: Shirts - Yellow with Blue Sleeves
Former Name(s): None	Shorts - Blue
Nickname: 'The Boro'	**Telephone No.**: (01252) 541469
Ground: John Roberts Ground, Cherrywood Road, Farnborough	**Daytime Phone No.**: (01252) 541469
	Pitch Size: 115 × 77yds
Record Attendance: 3,581 (vs Brentford 1995)	**Ground Capacity**: 4,900
	Seating Capacity: 500

GENERAL INFORMATION
Supporters Club Administrator: Paul Doe
Address: c/o Club
Telephone Number: (01252) 541469
Car Parking: Car Park at Ground
Coach Parking: At Ground
Nearest Railway Station: Farnborough (Main), Farnborough North & Frimley
Nearest Bus Station: –
Club Shop: Yes
Opening Times: Matchdays Only
Telephone No.: –
Postal Sales: Via Club
Nearest Police Station: Farnborough
Police Force: Hampshire
Police Telephone No.: (01252) 24545

GROUND INFORMATION
Away Supporters' Entrances: Moor Road
Away Supporters' Sections: Moor Road End

DISABLED SUPPORTERS INFORMATION
Wheelchairs: Accommodated in front of Main Stand
Disabled Toilets: Yes
Contact Nº: (01252) 541469

ADMISSION INFO (1997/98 PRICES)
Adult Standing: £6.00
Adult Seating: £7.00
Child Standing: £4.00
Child Seating: £5.00
Programme Price: £1.20
FAX Number: (01252) 375613

```
            COVERED TERRACES
  M                                  P
  O   ┌──────────────────────────┐   R
  O   │  ┌───┐          ┌───┐  │   O
  R   │  │   │    ◯     │   │  │   S
      │  └───┘          └───┘  │   P
  R   │                          │   E
  O   │                          │   C
  A   │                          │   T
  D   │                          │
      │                          │   R
  E   │                          │   O
  N   └──────────────────────────┘   A
  D                                  D
            MAIN STAND               E
                                     N
                                     D
```

Travelling Supporters Information:
Routes: Exit M3 junction 4 heading for Frimley. At Roundabout take A331 towards Farnborough. At Traffic Lights, turn right into Prospect Avenue and then take 2nd right into Cherrywood Road for the Ground.

GATESHEAD FC

Founded: 1930 (Reformed 1977) **Former Name(s)**: Gateshead United **Nickname**: 'Tynesiders' **Ground**: International Stadium, Neilson Road, Gateshead NE10 0EF **Record Attendance**: 11,750 vs Newcastle United (1995)	**Colours**: Shirts - Black & White Halves Shorts - Black **Telephone No.**: (0191) 478-3883 **Daytime Phone No.**: (0191) 478-3883 **Pitch Size**: 110 × 70yds **Ground Capacity**: 11,750 **Seating Capacity**: 11,750

GENERAL INFORMATION

Supporters Club Administrator:
Tommy Doleman
Address: 3 Frazer Terrace, Gateshead, Tyne
& Wear   NE10 0YA
Telephone Number: (0191) 469-2688
Car Parking: At Stadium
Coach Parking: At Stadium
Nearest Railway Station: Gateshead Stadium
Metro (0.5 mile); Newcastle (B.R.) 1.5 miles
Nearest Bus Station: Gateshead Interchange
(1 mile)
Club Shop: Yes – At Stadium
Opening Times: Matchdays Only
Telephone No.: (0191) 478-3883
Postal Sales: Yes
Nearest Police Station: Gateshead
Police Force: Northumbria
Police Telephone No.: (0191) 232-3451

GROUND INFORMATION

Away Supporters' Entrances: Tyne & Wear Stand
North End
Away Supporters' Sections: Tyne & Wear Stand
North End

DISABLED INFORMATION

Wheelchairs: 5 spaces each for Home & Away fans by
the trackside
Disabled Toilets: Available in the Reception Area and
on 1st floor Concourse
Contact Nº: (0191) 478-3883

ADMISSION INFO (1997/98 PRICES)

Adult Seating: £6.00
Child Seating: £3.00
Programme Price: £1.20
FAX Number: (0191) 477-1315

TYNE & WEAR
COUNTY STAND

SOUTH TERRACE

NORTH TERRACE

EAST STAND TERRACE

Travelling Supporters Information:
Routes: Take A1(M) to end of Motorway, just north of Washington (Birtley Services). Fork right (A194M)
to the end then turn left at the roundabout on to the A184. The stadium is 3 miles on the right.

HALIFAX TOWN FC

Founded: 1911
Turned Professional: 1911
Limited Company: 1911
Admitted to League: 1921
Former Name(s): None
Nickname: 'Shaymen'
Ground: Shay Ground, Shay Syke, Halifax HX1 2YS

Record Attendance: 36,885 (14/2/53)
Colours: Shirts - Blue & White Stripes
Shorts - Black
Telephone No.: (01422) 345543
Daytime Phone No.: (01422) 345543
Pitch Size: 110 × 75yds
Ground Capacity: 5,194
Seating Capacity: 1,896

GENERAL INFORMATION
Supporters Club Administrator: Secretary, Stephen Kell
Address: Halifax Town Promotions, c/o Club
Telephone Number: (01422) 353423
Car Parking: Shaw Hill Car Park (Nearby)
Coach Parking: Calderdale Bus Depot (Shaw Hill)
Nearest Railway Station: Halifax (3 minutes walk)
Nearest Bus Station: Halifax (10 mins. walk)
Club Shop: Westgate, Halifax
Opening Times: Weekdays 10.00am–5.00pm (Except Fridays) & Matchdays 10.00–2.30pm
Telephone No.: (01422) 353423
Postal Sales: Yes
Nearest Police Station: Halifax (1.25 miles)
Police Force: West Yorkshire
Police Telephone No.: (01422) 360333

GROUND INFORMATION
Away Supporters' Entrances: Shay Syke turnstiles
Away Supporters' Sections: Visitor's enclosure, Shay Syke

DISABLED INFORMATION
Wheelchairs: 10 spaces available in total in Disabled Stand
Disabled Toilets: At end of ramp from the Stand
Contact Nº: (01422) 345543

ADMISSION INFO (1997/98 PRICES)
Adult Standing: £7.00
Adult Seating: £7.00
Child Standing: £4.00 (Under 12' £1.00)
Child Seating: £4.00
Programme Price: £1.50
FAX Number: (01422) 349487

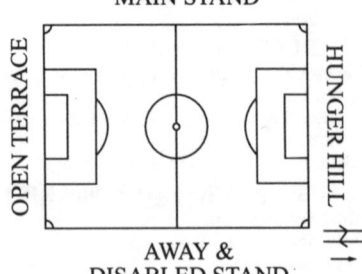

Huddersfield Road (A629)
MAIN STAND

OPEN TERRACE

HUNGER HILL

AWAY &
DISABLED STAND

Travelling Supporters Information:
Routes: From North: Take A629 to Halifax Town Centre. Take 2nd exit at roundabout into Broad Street and follow signs for Huddersfield (A629) into Skircoat Road; From South, East & West: Exit M62 junction 24 and follow Halifax (A629) signs to Town Centre into Skircoat Road for Ground.

HAYES FC

Founded: 1909	**Colours**: Shirts - Red & White Stripes
Former Name(s): Botwell Mission	Shorts - Black
Nickname: 'The Missioners'	**Telephone No.**: (0181) 573-2075
Ground: Church Road, Hayes, Middlesex	**Daytime Phone No.**: (0181) 575-0271
Record Attendance: 15,370 vs Bromley	**Pitch Size**: 117 × 70yds
(10/2/51)	**Ground Capacity**: 6,500
	Seating Capacity: 450

GENERAL INFORMATION

Supporters Club Administrator: Lee Hermitage
Address: c/o Hayes FC, Church Road
Telephone Number: (0181) 573-4598
Car Parking: 300 Cars at Ground
Coach Parking: By arrangement
Nearest Railway Station: Hayes & Harlington (1 mile)
Nearest Bus Station: Hayes
Club Shop: Yes
Opening Times: 2.00pm – 5.00pm Saturday matches;   6.45 – 9.30pm Midweek matches
Telephone No.: (0181) 573-5342
Postal Sales: Address to Lee Hermitage, c/o Hayes FC
Nearest Police Station: Hayes End (Morgans Lane)
Police Force: Metropolitan
Police Telephone No.: (0181) 900-7212

GROUND INFORMATION

Away Supporters' Entrances: No Segregation Usual
Away Supporters' Sections: but may be segregated at Church Road End.

DISABLED INFORMATION

Wheelchairs: No specific area, but accommodated as necessary
Disabled Toilets: Yes
Contact Nº: (0181) 573-2075

ADMISSION INFO (1997/98 PRICES)

Adult Standing: £6.00
Adult Seating: £7.00
Child Standing: £4.00
Child Seating: £5.00
Programme Price: £1.20
FAX Number: (0181) 573-2075

COVERED STANDING

UNCOVERED

GRANDSTAND

CAR PARK CHURCH ROAD

Travelling Supporters Information:
Routes: From A40: Approaching London, take Ruislip junction - turn right onto B455 Ruislip Road to White Hart Roundabout. Take Hayes by-pass to Uxbridge Road (A4020), turn right, then Church Road is 0.75 mile on the left, opposite Adam & Eve Pub. From M4: Exit junction 3 and take A312 to Parkway towards Southall, then Hayes by-pass to Uxbridge Road (A4020). Turn left, then as above.

HEDNESFORD TOWN FC

Founded: 1880
Former Name(s): Club formed by amalgamation of West Hill & Hill Top in 1880
Nickname: 'The Pitmen'
Ground: Keys Park, Hill Street, Hednesford
Record Attendance: 3,500 vs Wolverhampton Wanderers (Sep 1995)

Colours: Shirts - White
Shorts - Black
Telephone No.: (01543) 422870
Daytime Phone No.: (01543) 422870
Pitch Size: 115 × 74yds
Ground Capacity: 3,500
Seating Capacity: 730

GENERAL INFORMATION
Supporters Club Administrator: John Rafferty
Address: c/o Club
Telephone Number: (01543) 422870
Car Parking: Space for 500 cars at ground
Coach Parking: Available at ground
Nearest Railway Station: Hednesford (1 ml)
Nearest Bus Station: Hednesford
Club Shop: Yes
Opening Times: 10.00am – 4.00pm Monday to Friday & Matchdays
Telephone No.: (01543) 422870
Postal Sales: Yes
Nearest Police Station: Hednesford
Police Force: Staffordshire
Police Telephone No.: (01543) 574545

GROUND INFORMATION
Away Supporters' Entrances: Hednesford End – If required
Away Supporters' Sections: Hednesford End – If required

DISABLED INFORMATION
Wheelchairs: 20 spaces available in total in front of the Main Stand
Disabled Toilets: 2 available – One in Main Building and one in Hednesford End of Stand
Contact Nº: (01543) 422870

ADMISSION INFO (1997/98 PRICES)
Adult Standing: £6.50
Adult Seating: £7.50
Child Standing: £3.50
Child Seating: £4.50
Programme Price: £1.30
FAX Number: (01543) 428180

HEDNESFORD END

HEATH HAYES END

MAIN STAND

Travelling Supporters Information:
Routes: Exit M6 at junction 11 to Cannock and follow A460 towards Hednesford. After 2 miles turn right opposite the Shell Garage, ground is at bottom of hill on left.

HEREFORD UNITED FC

Founded: 1924
Former Name(s): None
Nickname: United & The Bulls
Ground: Edgar Street, Hereford, HR4 9JU
Record Attendance: 18,114 (4/1/58)
Colours: Shirts - White
Shorts - Black

Telephone No.: (01432) 276666
Daytime Phone No.: (01432) 276666
Pitch Size: 111 × 74yds
Ground Capacity: 8,843
Seating Capacity: 2,761

GENERAL INFORMATION
Supporters Club Administrator:
K.Benjimen
Address: c/o Club
Telephone Number: (01432) 276666
Car Parking: Merton Meadow & Edgar Street Car Parks
Coach Parking: Cattle Market (Near Ground)
Nearest Railway Station: Hereford (0.5 mile)
Nearest Bus Station: Commercial Road, Hereford
Club Shop: At Ground
Opening Times: Matchdays & Weekdays via Commercial Office
Telephone No.: (01432) 276666
Postal Sales: Yes
Nearest Police Station: Bath Street, Hereford
Police Telephone No.: (01432) 276422

GROUND INFORMATION
Away Supporters' Entrances: Blackfriars Street & Edgar Street
Away Supporters' Sections: Blackfriars Street End

DISABLED INFORMATION
Wheelchairs: 10 spaces each for home & away fans in Disabled section, Edgar Street Side
Disabled Toilets: None
Contact Nº: (01432) 276666

ADMISSION INFO (1997/98 PRICES)
Adult Standing: £7.00
Adult Seating: £9.00 – £10.00
Child Standing: £2.00 – £3.00
Child Seating: £5.00 – £6.00
Programme Price: £1.50
FAX Number: (01432) 341359

MERTON MEADOW STANDS

MERTON MEADOW TERRACES

BLACK FRIARS STREET (Away)

EDGAR STREET

Travelling Supporters Information:
Routes: From the North: Follow A49 Hereford signs straight into Edgar Street; From East: Take A465 or A438 into Hereford Town Centre, then follow signs for Leominster (A49) into Edgar Street; From South: Take A49 of A45 into Town Centre (then as East); From West: Take A438 into the Town Centre (then as East).

KETTERING TOWN FC

Founded: 1872	**Colours**: Shirts - Red
Former Name(s): None	Shorts - Red
Nickname: 'The Poppies'	**Telephone No.**: (01536) 483028/410815
Ground: Rockingham Road, Kettering,	**Daytime Phone No.**: (01536) 483028
Northants	**Pitch Size**: 110 × 70yds
Record Attendance: 11,526 vs Peterborough	**Ground Capacity**: 6,500
(1947-48)	**Seating Capacity**: 1,800

GENERAL INFORMATION
Supporters Trust Administrator: c/o Club
Address: –
Telephone Number: –
Car Parking: At Ground
Coach Parking: Cattle Market, Northfield Avenue, Kettering
Nearest Railway Station: Kettering (1 mile)
Nearest Bus Station: Kettering (1 mile)
Club Shop: At Ground. Also at Ken Burton's Sports Shop in Silver Street, Kettering
Opening Times: Shop hours in Town Centre, Matchdays and on request at the Ground
Telephone No.: (01536) 483028
Postal Sales: Yes
Nearest Police Station: London Road, Kettering
Police Force: Northants
Police Telephone No.: (01536) 411411

GROUND INFORMATION
Away Supporters' Entrances: Rockingham Road
Away Supporters' Sections: Rockingham Road End

DISABLED INFORMATION
Wheelchairs: 12 spaces available in total on terracing adjacent to the Main Stand
Disabled Toilets: Next to the Social Club
Contact Nº: (01536) 483028

ADMISSION INFO (1997/98 PRICES)
Adult Standing: £6.00
Adult Seating: £8.00
Child Standing: £5.00
Child Seating: £6.00
Programme Price: £1.30
FAX Number: (01536) 412273

BRITANNIA ROAD

COWPER STREET

ROCKINGHAM ROAD (Away)

MAIN STAND

Travelling Supporters Information:
Routes: To reach Kettering from the A1, M1 or M6, use the A14 to Junction 7, follow A43 for 1 mile, turn right at roundabout and Ground is 400 yards on left on A6003. (The Ground is situated to the North of Kettering (1 mile) on the main A6003 Rockingham Road to Oakham).

KIDDERMINSTER HARRIERS FC

Founded: 1886
Former Name(s): None
Nickname: 'Harriers'
Ground: Aggborough, Hoo Road, Kidderminster, Worcestershire
Record Attendance: 9,155 vs Hereford United (1948)

Colours: Shirts - Red & White Halves
Shorts - Red
Telephone No.: (01562) 823931
Pitch Size: 110 × 72yds
Ground Capacity: 6,200
Seating Capacity: 1,100

GROUND INFORMATION
Away Supporters' Entrances: South Entrance
Away Supporters' Sections: South Stand

DISABLED INFORMATION
Wheelchairs: Accommodated at front of Main Stand
Disabled Toilets: Available by the disabled area
Contact Nº: (01562) 823931

ADMISSION INFO (1997/98 PRICES)
Adult Standing: £6.00
Adult Seating: £8.00
Child Standing: £3.00
Child Seating: £5.00
Programme Price: £1.50
FAX Number: (01562) 827329
Junior Supporters Under 14's Club-Members: £12.00 per season
Under 16's: £27.00 per season

GENERAL INFORMATION
Supporters Club Administrator: C. Wood (Secretary)
Address: Kidderminster Harriers Social & Supporters Club, Stadium Close, Kidderminster
Telephone Number: (01562) 740198
Car Parking: At Ground
Coach Parking: At Ground
Nearest Railway Station: Kidderminster
Nearest Bus Station: Kidderminster Town Centre
Club Shop: Yes
Opening Times: Weekdays 9.00am–5.00pm & First Team Matchdays
Telephone No.: (01562) 823931
Postal Sales: Yes
Nearest Police Station: Habberley Road, Kidderminster
Police Force: West Mercia
Police Telephone No.: (01562) 820888

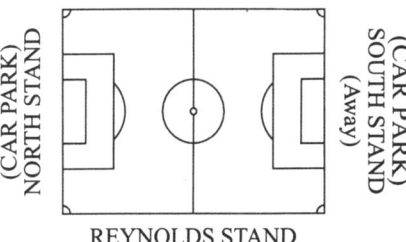

BILL GREAVES STAND

(CAR PARK) NORTH STAND

(CAR PARK) SOUTH STAND (Away)

REYNOLDS STAND (HOO ROAD)

Travelling Supporters Information:
Routes: From North: Exit M5 (junction 3) and take A456 to Kidderminster. Turn left at the traffic lights (A449 Worcester) then through the next set of traffic lights and under the railway viaduct to the traffic island. Turn right round the island and take 1st left 100 yards into Hoo Road; From South: Exit M5 (junction 6) and take A449 to Kidderminster. Turn right at the first traffic island approaching the town centre. Take first left into Hoo Road; Alternative Route: Exit M42 at junction 1 and take A38 to Bromsgrove and A448 to Kidderminster. At the first traffic island on town approach turn left into Spennells Valley Road. Straight on at the next traffic island, under the railway viaduct, then as North.

LEEK TOWN FC

Founded: 1946
Former Name(s): Abbey Green Rovers; Leek Lowe Hamil
Nickname: 'Blues'
Ground: Harrison Park, Macclesfield Road, Leek, Staffs ST13 8LD
Record Attendance: 5,312 vs Macclesfield Tn. (1973/74)

Colours: Shirts - Blue
Shorts - Blue
Telephone No.: (01538) 399278
Pitch Size: 115 × 80yds
Ground Capacity: 3,700
Seating Capacity: 640

GENERAL INFORMATION
Supporters Club Administrator: Brian Corden
Address: c/o Club
Telephone Number: (01538) 399278
Car Parking: 80 Cars at Ground
Coach Parking: At Ground
Nearest Railway Station: Stoke or Macclesfield (both 13 miles)
Nearest Bus Station: Leek
Club Shop: Yes
Opening Times: Matchdays & Weekdays
Telephone No.: (01538) 399278
Postal Sales: Yes
Nearest Police Station: Leek
Police Force: Staffordshire
Police Telephone No.: (01538) 399333

GROUND INFORMATION
Away Supporters' Entrances: Grace Street
Away Supporters' Sections: Grace Street Paddock

DISABLED INFORMATION
Wheelchairs: 5 spaces for home fans, 4 for away fans
Disabled Toilets: 2 available
Contact Nº: (01538) 399276

ADMISSION INFO (1997/98 PRICES)
Adult Standing: £6.00
Adult Seating: £7.00
Child Standing: £4.00
Child Seating: £5.00
Programme Price: £1.30
FAX Number: (01538) 399826

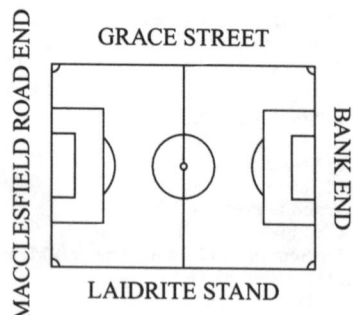

Travelling Supporters Information:
Routes: From North: Exit M6 at junction 17 to Macclesfield then follow A53 to Buxton Road; From South: Exit M6 at junction 15 to City Centre then follow A523 Leek Road. Ground is situated 0.5 mile outside Leek on Macclesfield side of the A523 Macclesfield to Buxton road.

MORECAMBE FC

Founded: 1920	**Colours**: Shirts - Red
Former Name(s): Woodhill Lane (1920)	Shorts - Black
Nickname: 'Shrimps'	**Telephone No.**: (01524) 411797
Ground: Christie Park, Lancaster Road,	**Daytime Phone No.**: (01524) 411797
Morecambe LA4 4TJ	**Pitch Size**: 118 × 76yds
Record Attendance: 9,324 vs Weymouth	**Ground Capacity**: 4,500
(1962)	**Seating Capacity**: 1,000

GENERAL INFORMATION
Supporters Club Administrator: −
Address: −
Telephone Number: −
Car Parking: At Ground
Coach Parking: At Ground
Nearest Railway Station: Morecambe Central (0.5 mile)
Nearest Bus Station: Morecambe
Club Shop: Yes
Opening Times: Mondays to Fridays & Matchdays 9.00am − 5.00pm
Telephone No.: (01524) 411797
Postal Sales: Yes
Nearest Police Station: Morecambe
Police Force: Lancashire
Police Telephone No.: (01524) 411534

GROUND INFORMATION
Away Supporters' Entrances: Corner of South Terrace and Lancaster Road
Away Supporters' Sections: South Terrace

DISABLED INFORMATION
Wheelchairs: 10 spaces available in total on approach to the Main Stand
Disabled Toilets: Yes
Contact Nº: (01524) 411797

ADMISSION INFO (1997/98 PRICES)
Adult Standing: £6.00
Adult Seating: £7.00
Child Standing: £3.00
Child Seating: £4.00
Programme Price: £1.20
FAX Number: (01524) 832230

MAIN STAND — Disabled Stand

SOUTH TERRACE — Away

NORTH TERRACE

LANCASTER ROAD

Travelling Supporters Information:
Routes: Exit M6 at junction 34. Then take A683 west in Lancaster and pick-up the A589 to Morecambe. At second roundabout on the outskirts of Morecambe, take 2nd exit into Lancaster Road and ground is on left, approximately 800 yards.

NORTHWICH VICTORIA FC

Founded: 1874
Former Name(s): None
Nickname: 'The Vics'
Ground: The Drill Field, Field Road, Northwich, Cheshire
Record Attendance: 11,290 vs Witton Albion (1949)

Colours: Shirts - Green
Shorts - White
Telephone No.: (01606) 41450
Daytime Phone No.: (01606) 41450
Pitch Size: 110 × 73yds
Ground Capacity: Currently 3,600
Seating Capacity: 660

GENERAL INFORMATION
Supporters Club Administrator: John Gleave
Address: c/o Club
Telephone Number: (01606) 41450
Car Parking: Street Parking
Coach Parking: Old Fire Station – adjacent
Nearest Railway Station: Northwich (1.5 miles)
Nearest Bus Station: 100 yards
Club Shop: At ground
Opening Times: Matchdays Only
Telephone No.: (01606) 41450
Postal Sales: Yes
Nearest Police Station: Chester Way, Northwich
Police Force: Cheshire
Police Telephone No.: (01606) 48000

GROUND INFORMATION
Away Supporters' Entrances: Terminus End
Away Supporters' Sections: Terminus End

DISABLED INFORMATION
Wheelchairs: Accommodated in front of Main Stand
Disabled Toilets: None
Contact Nº: (01606) 41450

ADMISSION INFO (1997/98 PRICES)
Adult Standing: £6.00
Adult Seating: £7.50
Child Standing: £4.00
Child Seating: £5.00
Programme Price: £1.20
FAX Number: (01606) 330577

DANE BANK

TERMINUS END (Away)

WATER STREET END

STAND

Travelling Supporters Information:
Routes: From North & South: Exit M6 junction 19 and take A556. Turn right at second roundabout (A559) and follow road for 1.5 miles - ground on right; From East & West: Take A556 to junction with A559, then as North.

RUSHDEN & DIAMONDS FC

Founded: 1992
Former Name(s): Rushden Town FC & Irthlingborough Diamonds FC
Nickname: 'Diamonds'
Ground: Nene Park, Irthlingborough, Northants
Record Attendance: 4,664 (vs Merthyr Tydfil, 1996)

Colours: Shirts - White with Red & Blue Trim
Shorts - Blue
Telephone No.: (01933) 652000
Daytime Phone No.: (01933) 652000
Pitch Size: 111 × 74yds
Ground Capacity: 6,635
Seating Capacity: 4,723

GENERAL INFORMATION
Supporters Club Administrator: Phil Wilton
Address: c/o Club
Telephone Number: (01933) 680035
Car Parking: At Ground
Coach Parking: At Ground
Nearest Railway Station: Wellingborough (5 miles)
Nearest Bus Station: Wellingborough
Club Shop: Yes – At the 'Doc' Shop
Opening Times: Weekdays and Matchdays 9.00am–5.00pm & Saturdays 10.00 – 5.30, Sundays 10.00 – 4.00pm
Telephone No.: (01933) 652000
Postal Sales: Yes
Nearest Police Station: Wellingborough
Police Force: Northamptonshire
Police Telephone No.: (01933) 440333

GROUND INFORMATION
Away Supporters' Entrances: Segregation if required
Away Supporters' Sections: Signposted

DISABLED INFORMATION
Wheelchairs: Accommodated around the ground
Disabled Toilets: Available in various parts of ground
Contact Nº: (01933) 652000

ADMISSION INFO (1997/98 PRICES)
Adult Standing: £6.00
Adult Seating: £7.00
Child Standing: £3.00
Child Seating: £4.00
Programme Price: £1.30
FAX Number: (01933) 650418

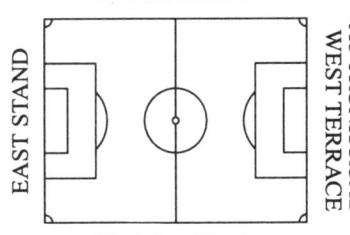

Travelling Supporters Information:
Routes: The ground is located on the A6 about 350 yards north of the junction with the A45 (over bridge).

SLOUGH TOWN FC

Founded: 1890
Limited Company: February 1992
Former Name(s): Slough, Slough United
Nickname: 'The Rebels'
Ground: Wexham Park Stadium, Wexham Road, Slough   SL2 5QR
Record Attendance: 5,000 (1982)

Colours: Shirts - Amber
Shorts - Navy Blue
Telephone No.: (01753) 523358
Daytime Phone No.: (01753) 523358
Pitch Size: 110 × 70yds
Ground Capacity: 5,000
Seating Capacity: 450

GENERAL INFORMATION
Supporters Association Administrator: Chris Sliski
Address: 143 Knolton Way, Slough
Telephone Number: (01753) 526891
Car Parking: Spaces for 460 cars at Ground
Coach Parking: 3 coach bays at Ground
Nearest Railway Station: Slough (2 miles)
Nearest Bus Station: Slough (2 miles)
Club Shop: Yes – Under the Stand
Opening Times: Daily
Telephone No.: (01753) 523358
Postal Sales: Yes
Nearest Police Station: Slough
Police Force: Thames Valley
Police Telephone No.: (01753) 506000

GROUND INFORMATION
Away Supporters' Entrances: North End to right of Clubhouse (Normally No Segregation)
Away Supporters' Sections: Golf Driving Range End /North End

DISABLED INFORMATION
Wheelchairs: 10 spaces each for home & away fans in front of the Main Stand
Disabled Toilets: One available inside the Clubhouse
Contact Nº: (01753) 523358

ADMISSION INFO (1997/98 PRICES)
Adult Standing: £7.00
Adult Seating: £7.00
Child Standing: £4.00   **Programme**: £1.50
Child Seating: £4.00   **Fax**: (01753) 516956

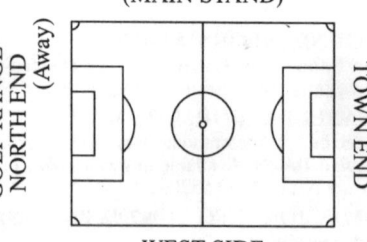

CLUBHOUSE
(MAIN STAND)

GOLF RANGE
NORTH END
(Away)

TOWN END

WEST SIDE

Travelling Supporters Information:
Routes: From North: Take the M25 to junction 16 and join M40. Exit at junction 1, Follow A412 (South) through Iver Heath to George Green. At the 2nd set of traffic lights turn right by the George Public House in George Green. Church Lane is 1 mile to the end, then turn left at the small roundabout and the ground is 0.25 mile on the right; From East: Take the M25 to junction 15 and join M4. Exit at junction 5 and follow A4 westbound as far as the Co-op Superstore on the right. Join A412 Northbound towards Uxbridge and follow the dual carriageway to the 4th set of traffic lights. Enter Church Lane, then as North; From South: (from Windsor Direction) Take A355 then onto the M4 and exit at junction 6 onto the A4. Turn right, pass Brunel Bus Station on left, Tesco Superstore, also on the left then turn first left into Wexham Road, signposted Wexham Park Hospital. Ground is just over 1 mile on the left; From West: Take M4 to junction 6 then follow route from South.

SOUTHPORT FC

Founded: 1881	**Colours**: Shirts - Old Gold
Former Name(s): Southport Vulcan FC;	Shorts - Black
Southport Central FC	**Telephone No.**: (01704) 533422
Nickname: 'The Sand Grounders'	**Daytime Phone No.**: (01704) 211428
Ground: Haig Avenue, Southport, Merseyside	**Pitch Size**: 115 × 78yds
Record Attendance: 20,010 vs Newcastle	**Ground Capacity**: 6,000
United (1932)	**Seating Capacity**: 1,880

GENERAL INFORMATION
Supporters Club Administrator:
Roy Morris
Address: 'Manikata', 3 Stretton Drive,
Southport
Telephone Number: (01704) 211428
Car Parking: Street Parking
Coach Parking: Adjacent to Ground
Nearest Railway Station: Southport (1.5 miles)
Nearest Bus Station: Town Centre
Club Shop: Yes
Opening Times: Matchdays 2.30pm (or 7.00pm) & also at Half-time. Fridays 7-9pm
Telephone No.: (01704) 533422
Postal Sales: Yes
Nearest Police Station: Southport
Police Force: Merseyside
Police Telephone No.: (0151) 709-6010

GROUND INFORMATION
Away Supporters' Entrances: Blowick End
Away Supporters' Sections: Blowick End Terrace

DISABLED INFORMATION
Wheelchairs: Accommodated in Blowick End of the Stand
Disabled Toilets: Available at Blowick End of Stand
Contact Nº: (01704) 533422

ADMISSION INFO (1997/98 PRICES)
Adult Standing: £5.50
Adult Seating: £6.50
Child Standing: £3.00
Child Seating: £3.50
Programme Price: £1.20
FAX Number: (0151) 448-1982

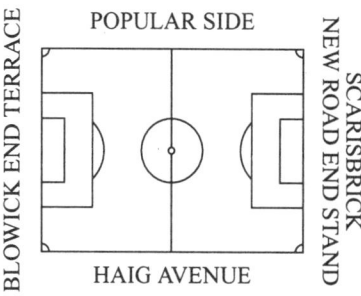

Travelling Supporters Information:
Routes: Exit M58 at junction 2 and take the A570 to Southport. At the first roundabout turn left into Scarisbrick New Road, pass over brook and turn right into Haig Avenue. Ground is on the right.

STALYBRIDGE CELTIC FC

Founded: 1909
Former Name(s): None
Nickname: 'Celtic'
Ground: Bower Fold, Mottram Road, Stalybridge, Cheshire
Record Attendance: 9,753 vs West Brom (1922/23)

Colours: Shirts - Blue & White Quarters
Shorts - Blue
Telephone No.: (0161) 338-2828
Daytime Phone No.: (0161) 338-2828
Pitch Size: 120 × 72yds
Ground Capacity: 6,000
Seating Capacity: 1,000

GENERAL INFORMATION
Supporters Club Administrator: John Hall
Address: 44 Chunal Lane, Glossop, Derbyshire SK13 9JX
Telephone Number: (01457) 869262
Car Parking: At Ground
Coach Parking: At Ground
Nearest Railway Station: Stalybridge (1 ml)
Nearest Bus Station: Stalybridge town centre
Club Shop: Yes
Opening Times: Monday–Friday & Saturday Matchdays 10.00am – 5.00pm
Telephone No.: (0161) 338-2828
Postal Sales: Yes
Nearest Police Station: Stalybridge Town Centre
Police Force: Greater Manchester
Police Telephone No.: (0161) 330-8321

GROUND INFORMATION
Away Supporters' Entrances: Mottram End (though not normally segregated)
Away Supporters' Sections: Mottram End

DISABLED INFORMATION
Wheelchairs: 20 spaces each for home & away fans in the Town End of the Main Stand
Disabled Toilets: 1 available at rear of the Main Stand
Contact Nº: (0161) 338-2828

ADMISSION INFO (1997/98 PRICES)
Adult Standing: £6.00
Adult Seating: £7.00
Child Standing: £4.00
Child Seating: £5.00
Programme Price: £1.30
FAX Number: (0161) 338-8256

MAIN STAND

JOE JACKSON STAND

MOTTRAM END (Away)

Travelling Supporters Information:
Routes: From the North: Take the M62 and exit at junction 19. Follow signs for Ashton-under-Lyne and then Stalybridge. Ground is approximately 1 mile through the town on the A6107 Mottram Road. From the Midlands and South: Take the M6, M56 and M67, leaving at the end of the motorway. Go across the roundabout to the traffic lights and turn left. The ground is approximately 2 miles on the left before the Hare & Hounds pub.

STEVENAGE BOROUGH FC

Founded: 1976	**Colours**: Shirts - White with Red Stripe
Former Name(s): None	Shorts - White
Nickname: 'Boro'	**Telephone No.**: (01438) 743322
Ground: Stevenage Stadium, Broadhall Way,	**Daytime Phone No.**: (01438) 743322
Stevenage, Herts SG2 8RH	**Pitch Size**: 110 × 70yds
Record Attendance: 6,489 vs Kidderminster	**Ground Capacity**: 6,546
Harriers (25/1/97)	**Seating Capacity**: 2,002

GENERAL INFORMATION
Supporters Club Administrator:
Mervyn Stoke Geddis
Address: 21 Woodland Way, Stevenage
Telephone Number: (01438) 313236
Car Parking: Spaces for 150 cars at ground and Fairlands Show Ground (opposite)
Coach Parking: At Ground
Nearest Railway Station: Stevenage (1 mile)
Nearest Bus Station: Stevenage
Club Shop: Yes
Opening Times: Matchdays Only
Telephone No.: (01438) 743322
Postal Sales: None
Nearest Police Station: Stevenage
Police Force: Hertfordshire
Police Telephone No.: (01438) 757000

GROUND INFORMATION
Away Supporters' Entrances: South Terrace
Away Supporters' Sections: South Terrace

DISABLED INFORMATION
Wheelchairs: Accommodated behind North Terrace
Disabled Toilets: Yes
Contact Nº: (01438) 743322

ADMISSION INFO (1997/98 PRICES)
Adult Standing: £7.00
Adult Seating: £8.00 − £12.00
Child Standing: £4.00
Child Seating: £5.00 − £7.00
Programme Price: £1.50
FAX Number: (01438) 743666
(Concessions for members)

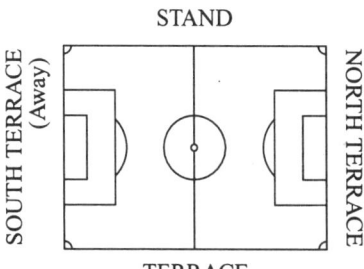

Travelling Supporters Information:
Routes: Exit A1(M) at junction 7 and take B197. Ground is on right at second roundabout.
Bus Routes: SB4 & SB5

TELFORD UNITED FC

Founded: 1877
Former Name(s): Wellington Town FC
Nickname: 'Lillywhites'
Ground: Bucks Head Ground, Watling Street, Wellington, Telford, Shropshire
Record Attendance: 13,000 vs Shrewsbury Town (1935)

Colours: Shirts - White
       Shorts - Blue
Telephone No.: (01952) 270767
Daytime Phone No.: (01952) 270767
Pitch Size: 110 × 75 yds
Ground Capacity: 4,600
Seating Capacity: 1,222

GENERAL INFORMATION
Supporters Club Administrator: The Secretary
Address: c/o Club
Telephone Number: (01952) 255662
Car Parking: At Ground
Coach Parking: At Ground
Nearest Railway Station: Wellington – Telford West
Nearest Bus Station: –
Club Shop: Yes
Opening Times: Matchdays Only
Telephone No.: (01952) 270767
Postal Sales: Yes
Nearest Police Station: Wellington
Police Force: West Mercia
Police Telephone No.: (01952) 290888

GROUND INFORMATION
Away Supporters' Entrances: North Bank Turnstiles
Away Supporters' Sections: North Bank

DISABLED INFORMATION
Wheelchairs: Accommodated at South End of Ground
Disabled Toilets: None
Contact Nº: (01952) 270767

ADMISSION INFO (1997/98 PRICES)
Adult Standing: £6.00
Adult Seating: £8.00
Child Standing: £4.00
Child Seating: £4.00 & £5.00
Programme Price: £1.30
FAX Number: (01952) 270776

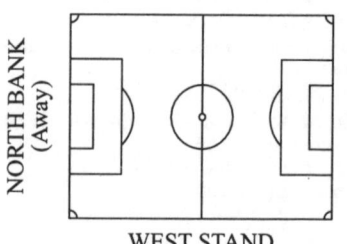

Travelling Supporters Information:
Routes: Exit M54 junction 6 and take A518 and B5061 to Wellington district of town. Ground is on B5061 – formerly the main A5.

WELLING UNITED FC

Founded: 1963
Former Name(s): None
Nickname: 'The Wings'
Ground: Park View Road Ground, Welling, Kent
Record Attendance: 4,020 (1989/90)

Colours: Shirts - Red with White facings
Shorts - Red
Telephone No.: (0181) 301-1196
Daytime Phone No.: (0181) 301-1196
Pitch Size: 112 × 72yds
Ground Capacity: 5,500
Seating Capacity: 500

GENERAL INFORMATION
Supporters Club Administrator: G. Youens
Address: c/o Club
Telephone Number: –
Car Parking: Street Parking Only
Coach Parking: Outside Ground
Nearest Railway Station: Welling (0.75 ml)
Nearest Bus Station: Bexleyheath
Club Shop: Yes
Opening Times: Matchdays Only
Telephone No.: (0181) 301-1196
Postal Sales: Yes
Nearest Police Station: Welling (0.5 mile)
Police Force: Metropolitan
Police Telephone No.: (0181) 304-3161

GROUND INFORMATION
Away Supporters' Entrances: -
Away Supporters' Sections: Danson Park End

DISABLED INFORMATION
Wheelchairs: Accommodated at side of Main Stand
Disabled Toilets: Yes
Contact Nº: (0181) 301-1196

ADMISSION INFO (1997/98 PRICES)
Adult Standing: £6.00
Adult Seating: £8.00
Child Standing: £4.00
Child Seating: £5.00
Programme Price: £1.20
FAX Number: (0181) 301-5676

CRICKET GROUND STAND

PARK VIEW ROAD END

DANSON PARK END (Away)

MAIN STAND

Travelling Supporters Information:
Routes: Take A2 (Rochester Way) from London, then A221 Northwards (Danson Road) to Bexleyheath. At end turn left towards Welling along Park View Road. Ground on left.

WOKING FC

Founded: 1889
Former Name(s): None
Nickname: 'Cardinals'
Ground: Kingfield Sports Ground, Kingsfield Road, Woking, Surrey GU22 9AA
Record Attendance: 6,000 vs Coventry City (1997)

Colours: Shirts - Red & White Halves
Shorts - Black
Telephone No.: (01483) 772470
Daytime Phone No.: (01483) 772470
Pitch Size: 113 × 70yds
Ground Capacity: 6,000
Seating Capacity: 2,500

GENERAL INFORMATION
Supporters Club Administrator: Secretary, Mr. A. Barnes
Address: c/o Club
Telephone Number: (01483) 772470
Car Parking: Spaces for 150 cars at Ground
Coach Parking: At or opposite Ground
Nearest Railway Station: Woking (1 mile)
Nearest Bus Station: Woking
Club Shop: Yes
Opening Times: All Week & Matchdays
Telephone No.: (01483) 772470
Postal Sales: Yes
Nearest Police Station: Woking
Police Force: Surrey
Police Telephone No.: (01483) 761991

GROUND INFORMATION
Away Supporters' Entrances: Kingfield Road or Westfield Avenue (if segregation in force)

DISABLED INFORMATION
Wheelchairs: 8 spaces in Leslie Gosden Stand + 8 spaces by the Club Shop
Disabled Toilets: Yes – in the Leslie Gosden Stand
Contact Nº: (01483) 772470

ADMISSION INFO (1997/98 PRICES)
Adult Standing: £7.00
Adult Seating: £7.00
Child/OAP Standing: £5.00
Child/OAP Seating: £5.00
Programme Price: £1.20
FAX Number: (01483) 888423
Note: Children under 11 are £2.00 with an adult

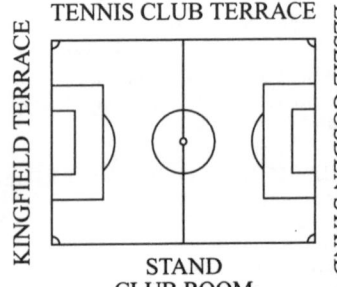

Travelling Supporters Information:
Routes: Exit M25 junction 10 and follow A30 towards Guildford, leave at next junction on B2215 through Ripley to join A247 to Woking OR Exit M25 junction 11 and follow A320 to Woking Town Centre, Ground on outskirts - follow signs on A320 then A247.

YEOVIL TOWN FC

Founded: 1923
Former Name(s): Yeovil & Petters United FC
Nickname: 'Glovers'
Ground: Huish Park Stadium, Lufton Way, Yeovil, Somerset BA22 8YF
Record Attendance: 8,618 vs Arsenal (2/1/93)

Colours: Shirts - Green & White Stripes
Shorts - White
Telephone No.: (01935) 423662
Daytime Phone No.: (01935) 423662
Pitch Size: 115 × 72yds
Ground Capacity: 8,820
Seating Capacity: 5,212

GENERAL INFORMATION
Supporters Club Administrator: G. Coggen
Address: c/o Club
Telephone Number: (01935) 434022
Car Parking: Parking for 1000 cars at Ground
Coach Parking: At Ground
Nearest Railway Station: Yeovil Pen Mill (2.5 miles); Yeovil Junction (3.5 miles)
Nearest Bus Station: Yeovil (2 miles)
Club Shop: Yes
Opening Times: Monday to Friday 10.00am – 12.30pm + most evenings & Matchdays
Telephone No.: (01935) 423662
Postal Sales: Yes
Nearest Police Station: Yeovil
Police Force: Avon & Somerset
Police Telephone No.: (01935) 415291
Conference Centre: (01935) 414094
Commercial Office: (01935) 479777

GROUND INFORMATION
Away Supporters' Entrances: Copse Road
Away Supporters' Sections: Visitors End

DISABLED INFORMATION
Wheelchairs: 8 spaces each for home and away fans
Disabled Toilets: 2 available
Contact Nº: (01935) 423662

ADMISSION INFO (1997/98 PRICES)
Adult Standing: £6.00
Adult Seating: £7.00
Child Standing: £3.00
Child Seating: £4.00
(Family Tickets are available at discounted rates)
Programme Price: £1.50
FAX Number: (01935) 473956

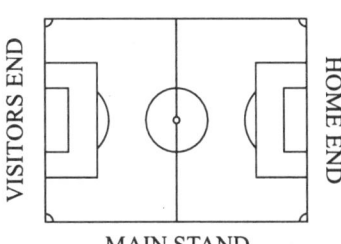

BARTLETT STAND

VISITORS END

HOME END

MAIN STAND

Travelling Supporters Information:
Routes: From London: Take M3 and A303 to Cartgate Roundabout. Enter Yeovil on A3088. Take 1st exit at next roundabout & straight across next roundabout into Western Avenue, cross next roundabout then turn left into Copse Road, where supporters parking is sited; From North: Exit M5 Junction 25 and take A358 (Ilminster) and A303 (Eastbound) entering Yeovil on A3088, then follow directions as London.

AYLESBURY UNITED FC

Founded: 1897
Former Name(s): None
Nickname: 'The Ducks'
Ground: The Stadium, Buckingham Road, Aylesbury, Bucks, HP20 2AQ
Record Attendance: 6,031 vs England (1988)

Colours: Shirts - Green
Shorts - Green
Telephone No.: (01296) 436350
Daytime Phone No.: (01296) 436350
Pitch Size: 112 × 74yds
Ground Capacity: 4,000
Seating Capacity: 400

GENERAL INFORMATION
Supporters Club Administrator:
The Secretary
Address: c/o Club
Telephone Number: (01296) 436350
Car Parking: 250 Cars at Ground
Coach Parking: At Ground
Nearest Railway Station: Aylesbury Town (20 minutes walk)
Nearest Bus Station: Aylesbury Bus Station (20 minutes walk)
Club Shop: At Ground
Opening Times: Matchdays & Office Hours
Telephone No.: (01296) 436350
Postal Sales: Yes
Nearest Police Station: Aylesbury
Police Force: Thames Valley
Police Telephone No.: (01296) 396000

GROUND INFORMATION
Away Supporters' Entrances: Country End
Away Supporters' Sections: Country End

DISABLED INFORMATION
Wheelchairs: Accommodated
Disabled Toilets: 1 Gents and 1 Ladies in Clubhouse
Contact Nº: (01296) 436350

ADMISSION INFO (1997/98 PRICES)
Adult Standing: £5.00
Adult Seating: £6.00
Child Standing: £3.00
Child Seating: £4.00
Programme Price: £1.50
FAX Number: (01296) 395667

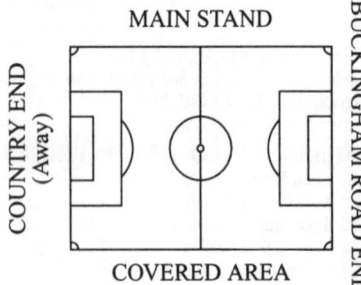

Travelling Supporters Information:
Routes: From Buckingham Direction: On outskirts of town, on left; From all other directions: Follow signs A413 Buckingham, ground on outskirts of town on right.

BASINGSTOKE TOWN FC

Founded: 1896	**Colours**: Shirts - Blue & Gold Stripes
Former Name(s): None	Shorts - Blue
Nickname: 'Stoke'	**Telephone No.**: (01256) 325063
Ground: The Camrose Ground, Western Way,	**Social Club Phone No.**: (01256) 464353
Basingstoke, Hants, RG22 6EZ	**Pitch Size**: 110 × 70yds
Record Attendance: 4,023 vs Torquay United	**Ground Capacity**: 5,000
(1989)	**Seating Capacity**: 750

GENERAL INFORMATION
Supporters Club Administrator: –
Address: c/o Club
Telephone Number: (01256) 325063
Car Parking: 600 Cars at Ground
Coach Parking: Ample room provided
Nearest Railway Station: Basingstoke
Nearest Bus Station: Basingstoke Town
Centre (2 miles)
Club Shop: Yes
Opening Times: Matchdays Only
Telephone No.: (01256) 325063
Postal Sales: Yes
Nearest Police Station: Basingstoke Town
Centre
Police Force: Hampshire
Police Telephone No.: (01256) 473111

GROUND INFORMATION
Away Supporters' Entrances: No usual segregation
Away Supporters' Sections: No usual segregation

DISABLED INFORMATION
Wheelchairs: Area available for wheelchairs
Disabled Toilets: None
The Blind: No special facilities

ADMISSION INFO (1997/98 PRICES)
Adult Standing: £4.50
Adult Seating: £5.00
Child Standing: £2.50
Child Seating: £3.00
Programme Price: £1.00
FAX Number: (01256) 473299
Under 16's: £1.00

MANSFIELD ROAD

COVERED TERRACE

WINCHESTER ROAD

Travelling Supporters Information:
Routes: Exit M3 at Junction 6, take 1st left at the Black Dam roundabout. At the next roundabout take the 2nd exit, then the 1st exit at the following roundabout and the 5th exit at the final roundabout. This takes you into Western Way, the ground is 50 yards on the right.

BISHOPS STORTFORD FC

Founded: 1874
Former Name(s): None
Nickname: 'Blues' 'Bishops'
Ground: George Wilson Stadium, Rhodes Avenue, Bishops Stortford, Herts   CM23 3JN
Record Attendance: 6,000 vs Peterborough United (1972)

Colours: Shirts - Blue & White Stripes
Shorts - Blue
Telephone No.: (01279) 654140
Secretary: (01279) 465998
Pitch Size: 112 × 78yds
Ground Capacity: 4,500
Seating Capacity: 300

GENERAL INFORMATION
Supporters Club Administrator: John Griggs
Address: c/o Club
Telephone Number: –
Car Parking: At Ground
Coach Parking: At Ground
Nearest Railway Station: Bishop's Stortford (10 minutes walk)
Nearest Bus Station: Bishop's Stortford (10 minutes walk)
Club Shop: Yes
Opening Times: Matchdays Only
Telephone No.: (01279) 658536
Postal Sales: Yes
Nearest Police Station: Bishop's Stortford
Police Force: Hertfordshire Constabulary
Police Telephone No.: –

GROUND INFORMATION
Away Supporters' Entrances: No Segregation
Away Supporters' Sections: No Segregation

DISABLED INFORMATION
Wheelchairs: Accommodated in front of Clubhouse Stand
Disabled Toilets: None
Contact Nº: (01279) 654140

ADMISSION INFO (1997/98 PRICES)
Adult Standing: £5.00
Adult Seating: £5.50
Child Standing: £3.00
Child Seating: £3.00
Programme Price: £1.00
FAX Number: (01279) 656538

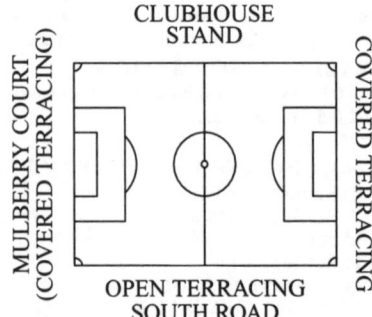

Travelling Supporters Information:
Routes: Exit M11 Junction 11 and take A120 towards town centre. Turn right at crossroads onto A1184 (London Road) then right again at mini-roundabout. Cross railway bridge then turn right at next roundabout (next to garage) and then 2nd left into Rhodes Avenue for the ground.

BOREHAM WOOD FC

Founded: 1946
Former Name(s): Boreham Rovers FC and Royal Retournez FC
Nickname: 'The Wood'
Ground: Meadow Park, Broughinge Road, Boreham Wood, Hertfordshire
Record Attendance: 2,500 vs St. Albans City (1971)

Colours: Shirts - White
Shorts - Black
Telephone No.: (0181) 953-5097
Contact Phone No.: (01923) 856077
Pitch Size: 112 × 72yds
Ground Capacity: 3,500
Seating Capacity: 400

GENERAL INFORMATION
Supporters Club Administrator: None
Address: –
Telephone Number: –
Car Parking: At Ground
Coach Parking: At Ground
Nearest Railway Station: Elstree & Boreham Wood (0.5 mile)
Nearest Bus Station: Barnet
Club Shop: Yes
Opening Times: Matchdays Only
Telephone No.: (0181) 953-5097
Postal Sales: –
Nearest Police Station: Boreham Wood (0.25 mile)
Police Force: Metropolitan
Police Telephone No.: (0181) 733-5024

GROUND INFORMATION
Away Supporters' Entrances: No Segregation
Away Supporters' Sections: No Segregation

DISABLED INFORMATION
Wheelchairs: Accommodated
Disabled Toilets: –
Contact Nº: (01923) 856077

ADMISSION INFO (1997/98 PRICES)
Adult Standing: £5.00
Adult Seating: £5.00
Child Standing: £3.00
Child Seating: £3.00
Programme Price: £1.00
FAX Number: (0181) 953-9883

MAIN STAND

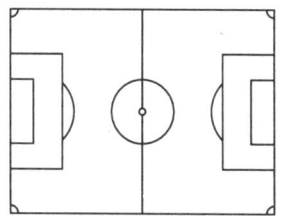

COVERED TERRACE

Travelling Supporters Information:
Routes: Exit M25 at Junction 23 and take A1 South. After 2-3 miles take Boreham Wood exit into Town. Turn right at the studio roundabout into Brook Road then next right into Broughinge Road for the Ground.

BROMLEY FC

Founded: 1892	**Colours**: Shirts - White
Former Name(s): None	Shorts - Black
Nickname: 'Lilywhites'	**Telephone No.**: (0181) 460-5291
Ground: Hayes Lane, Bromley, Kent	**Daytime Phone No.**: (0181) 313-3992 (Club)
Record Attendance: 12,000 vs Nigeria	**Pitch Size**: 112 × 78yds
(24/9/49)	**Ground Capacity**: 8,500
	Seating Capacity: 1,000

GENERAL INFORMATION
Supporters Club Administrator: Jack Freeman
Address: c/o Club
Telephone Number: (0181) 460-5291
Car Parking: 300 Cars at Ground
Coach Parking: At Ground
Nearest Railway Station: Bromley South (1 mile)
Nearest Bus Station: High Street, Bromley
Club Shop: Yes
Opening Times: Matchdays Only
Telephone No.: –
Postal Sales: Yes
Nearest Police Station: Widmore Road, Bromley
Police Force: Metropolitan 'P' Division (3 miles)
Police Telephone No.: (0181) 697-9212

GROUND INFORMATION
Away Supporters' Entrances: No Segregation
Away Supporters' Sections: No Segregation

DISABLED INFORMATION
Wheelchairs: Accommodated
Disabled Toilets: None
Contact Nº: (0181) 460-5291

ADMISSION INFO (1997/98 PRICES)
Adult Standing: £5.00
Adult Seating: £5.00
Child Standing: £3.00
Child Seating: £3.00
Programme Price: £1.00
FAX Number: (01474) 709495 (by arrangement)

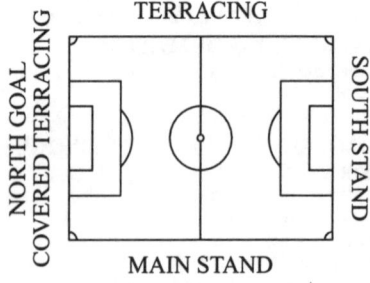

Travelling Supporters Information:
Routes: Exit M25 at A21 turnoff for Bromley and follow to A232 Croydon to Orpington Road. 1.5 miles past West Wickham (on Hayes Common), turn left into Baston Road (B265). Follow along into Hayes Street and then Hayes Lane. Ground is 0.5 mile along Hayes Lane on the right, set back from the road.

CARSHALTON ATHLETIC FC

Founded: 1905
Former Name(s): None
Nickname: 'The Robins'
Ground: War Memorial Sports Ground,
Colston Avenue, Carshalton, Surrey
Record Attendance: 7,800 vs Wimbledon

Colours: Shirts - White With Maroon Trim
Shorts - Maroon
Telephone No.: (0181) 770-3692
Daytime Phone No.: (01372) 272992
Pitch Size: 117 × 76yds
Ground Capacity: 8,000
Seating Capacity: 240

GENERAL INFORMATION
Supporters Club Administrator:
Sylvia Collier
Address: c/o Club
Telephone Number: (0181) 715-2229
Car Parking: Space for 80 Cars at Ground
Coach Parking: At Ground
Nearest Railway Station: Carshalton (200 yards)
Nearest Bus Station: 400 yards
Club Shop: Yes
Opening Times: Matchdays Only
Telephone No.: –
Postal Sales: Yes
Nearest Police Station: Sutton
Police Force: Metropolitan
Police Telephone No.: (0181) 680-6212

GROUND INFORMATION
Away Supporters' Entrances: No Segregation
Away Supporters' Sections: –

DISABLED INFORMATION
Wheelchairs: 6 spaces each for home & away fans accommodated at the end of the Stand
Disabled Toilets: None
Contact Nº: (0181) 770-3692

ADMISSION INFO (1997/98 PRICES)
Adult Standing: £5.00
Adult Seating: £5.50
Child Standing: £3.00
Child Seating: £3.50
Programme Price: £1.00
FAX Number: (0181) 770-3601

```
                COVERED TERRACE
                  (PARK SIDE)
        ┌──────────────────────────┐
  FLAT TERRACE                        CAR PARK & TURNSTILES
                                      COVERED TERRACE
        └──────────────────────────┘
                  MAIN STAND
```

Travelling Supporters Information:
Routes: From London: Pick up the A23 at The Elephant & Castle or The Oval. Continue along The Brixton Road (A23), through Brixton up Brixton Hill and continue past Streatham Hill to Streatham High Road (still on the A23). At the traffic lights on the junction at St.Leonard's Church, cross into Mitcham Lane (A216), continue through Streatham Road and bear left at the traffic lights at Figgs Marsh onto London Road (A217) and follow A217 through Bishopsford Road until reaching the Rose Hill roundabout. At roundabout take 1st exit into Wrythe Lane and continue for 1 mile, then turn right into Colston Avenue just before railway bridge. Ground 150 yards on right. A Private road leads to the Stadium and Car park; From the M25: Exit junction 8 on to A217 passing Lower Kingswood, Kingswood Burgh Heath, Banstead until roundabout before sign to Sutton. Bear left, still on the A217 until the Rose Hill roundabout is reached, take 4th exit then as above.

CHESHAM UNITED FC

Founded: 1887
Former Name(s): Chesham Generals FC & Chesham Town FC
Nickname: 'The Generals'
Ground: Meadow Park, Amy Lane, Chesham, Bucks, HP5 1NE
Record Attendance: 5,000 (5/12/79)

Colours: Shirts - Claret & Blue
　　　　　Shorts - Claret & Blue
Telephone No.: (01494) 783964
Daytime Phone No.: (01494) 783964
Pitch Size: 120 × 80yds
Ground Capacity: 5,000
Seating Capacity: 250

GENERAL INFORMATION
Supporters Club Administrator: Chris Spruytenburg
Address: c/o Club
Telephone Number: (01494) 783964
Car Parking: At Ground
Coach Parking: At Ground
Nearest Railway Station: Chesham (0.5 mile)
Nearest Bus Station: Chesham (10 mins.)
Club Shop: Yes
Opening Times: Matchdays Only
Telephone No.: (01494) 783964
Postal Sales: Yes
Nearest Police Station: Chesham Broad Street, Chesham
Police Force: Thames Valley
Police Telephone No.: (01494) 431133

GROUND INFORMATION
Away Supporters' Entrances: Segregation for special games only
Away Supporters' Sections: Segregation for special games only

DISABLED INFORMATION
Disabled Toilets: None

ADMISSION INFO (1997/98 PRICES)
Adult Standing: £5.00
Adult Seating: £6.00
Child Standing: £3.00 (Children under 6 – Free)
Child Seating: £4.00 (Children under 6 – Free)
Programme Price: £1.00
FAX Number: (01494) 791608

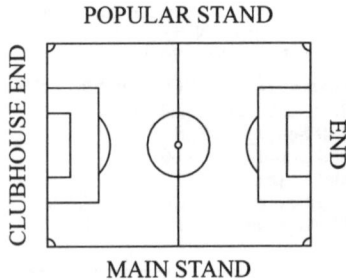

Travelling Supporters Information:
Routes: From Amersham: Take A416 to Chesham. Very sharp left at roundabout at foot of Amersham Road, into Meadow Park; From M25: Exit Junction 18. Take A404 to Amersham then as above; From M40: From West, exit Junction 4 and take A404 to Amersham then as above. Alternatively exit Junction 2 and take A355 to Amersham then as above.

DAGENHAM & REDBRIDGE FC

Founded: 1992
Former Name(s): Formed by merging of
Dagenham FC & Redbridge Forest FC
Nickname: 'The Daggers' / 'The Reds'
Ground: Victoria Road, Dagenham, Essex,
RM10 7XL
Record Attendance: 7,100 (1967)

Colours: Shirts - Red
   Shorts - Blue
Telephone No.: (0181) 592-1549
Office Phone No.: (0181) 592-7194
Secretary Phone No.: (0181) 524-2689
Pitch Size: 112 × 72yds
Ground Capacity: 5,500
Seating Capacity: 720

GENERAL INFORMATION
Supporters Club Administrator:
Russell Elmes
Address: 24 Brewood, Dagenham, RM8 2BL
Telephone Number: (0181) 593-2801
Car Parking: Car Park at Ground
Coach Parking: Car Park at Ground
Nearest Railway Station: Dagenham East
(5 minutes walk)
Nearest Bus Station: Romford
Club Shop: At Ground
Opening Times: Matchdays Only
Telephone No.: (0181) 592-7194
Postal Sales: Yes
Nearest Police Station: Dagenham East
Police Force: Metropolitan
Police Telephone No.: (0181) 593-8232

GROUND INFORMATION
Away Supporters' Entrances: Pondfield Road
Away Supporters' Sections: Pondfield End

DISABLED INFORMATION
Wheelchairs: 10 spaces available in South/West End
of the ground
Disabled Toilets: Available at East and West Ends.
Contact Nº: (0181) 592-7194

ADMISSION INFO (1997/98 PRICES)
Adult Standing: £5.00
Adult Seating: £7.00
Child Standing: £3.00
Child Seating: £7.00
Programme Price: £1.20
FAX Number: (0181) 593-7227

COVERED ACCOMMODATION

PONDFIELD END (Away)

VICTORIA ROAD END

MAIN STAND

(UNDERGROUND)

Travelling Supporters Information:
Routes: From West: Take A118 or A12 (Eastern Avenue) into Dagenham turning right into Whalebone
Lane. Branch left at Sports Arena into Wood Lane, then Rainham Road. After 0.5 mile turn right into Victoria
Road for Ground; From East: Take A118 or A12 (Eastern Avenue) into Dagenham turning left into Whale-
bone Lane (then as West); From North: Take B174 from Romford straight into Whalebone Lane (then as
West from Eastern Avenue).

DULWICH HAMLET FC

Founded: 1893
Former Name(s): None
Nickname: 'The Hamlet'
Ground: Champion Hill Stadium, Edgar Kail Way, London   SE22 8BD
Record Attendance: 1,604 vs Enfield (1996)

Colours: Shirts - Pink & Blue Stripes
Shorts - Blue
Telephone No.: (0171) 274-8707
Daytime Phone No.: (0171) 274-8707
Pitch Size: 110 × 70yds
Ground Capacity: 3,000
Seating Capacity: 500

GENERAL INFORMATION
Supporters Club Administrator: Mishi Morath
Address: c/o Club
Telephone Number: (0171) 274-8707
Car Parking: Space for 50 cars at ground
Coach Parking: At Ground
Nearest Railway Station: East Dulwich (adjacent)
Club Shop: Yes
Opening Times: Matchdays Only
Telephone No.: (0171) 274-8707
Postal Sales: Yes – c/o Club
Nearest Police Station: East Dulwich
Police Force: Metropolitan
Police Telephone No.: (0181) 693-3366

GROUND INFORMATION
Away Supporters' Entrances: No Segregation
Away Supporters' Sections: No Segregation

DISABLED INFORMATION
Wheelchairs: 10 spaces available in total in front of the Bar in the Stand Enclosure
Disabled Toilets: Easy access in the Club behind the disabled area
Contact Nº: (0171) 274-8707

ADMISSION INFO (1997/98 PRICES)
Adult Standing: £5.00
Adult Seating: £5.00
Child Standing: £3.00
Child Seating: £3.00
Programme Price: £1.00
FAX Number: (0171) 501-9255

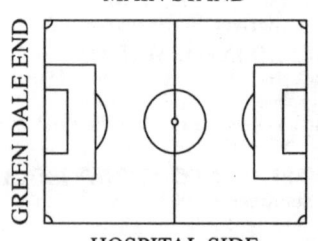

(SAINSBURY STORE)
MAIN STAND
GREEN DALE END
DOG KENNEL HILL END
HOSPITAL SIDE

Travelling Supporters Information:
Routes: From Elephant & Castle go down Walworth Road, through Camberwell's one-way system and along Denmark Hill. Turn left by the railway into Champion Park and then right at the end down Grave Lane to the ground in Dog Kennel Hill; From the South: Come up through Streatham on the A23, turn right to Tulse Hill along the A205 (Christchurch Road) and carry on towards Sydenham. Turn left at The Grove into Lordship Lane and carry on to East Dulwich.

ENFIELD FC

Founded: 1893	**Colours**: Shirts - White
Former Name(s): Enfield Spartans	Shorts - White
Nickname: -	**Telephone No.**: (0181) 292-0665
Ground: The Stadium, Southbury Road,	**Daytime Phone No.**: (0181) 292-0665
Enfield, Middlesex EN1 1YQ	**Pitch Size**: 118 × 74yds
Record Attendance: 10,000 vs Tottenham H.	**Ground Capacity**: 7,200
(10/10/62)	**Seating Capacity**: 675

GENERAL INFORMATION
Supporters Club Administrator:
Patrick Cunneen
Address: The Grumbles, Lackmore Road,
Enfield, Middlesex EN1 4PB
Telephone Number: (01992) 652415
Car Parking: Adjacent to Ground
Coach Parking: Adjacent to Ground
Nearest Railway Station: Enfield Town &
Southbury (both 800 yards)
Nearest Bus Station: Ponders End
Club Shop: Yes
Opening Times: Matchdays Only
Telephone No.: (0181) 292-0665
Postal Sales: Yes
Nearest Police Station: Enfield Town
Police Force: Metropolitan
Police Telephone No.: (0181) 367-2222

GROUND INFORMATION
Away Supporters' Entrances: Cambridge Road End
(Only when segregated)
Away Supporters' Sections: Cambridge Road End

DISABLED INFORMATION
Wheelchairs: 5 spaces each for home & away fans
adjacent to Starlight Suite
Disabled Toilets: None
Contact Nº: (0181) 292-0665

ADMISSION INFO (1997/98 PRICES)
Adult Standing: £5.00
Adult Seating: £6.00
Child Standing: £3.50
Child Seating: £6.00
Programme Price: £1.20
FAX Number: (0181) 292-0669
Note: Children under 11 are £2.00 when with an adult

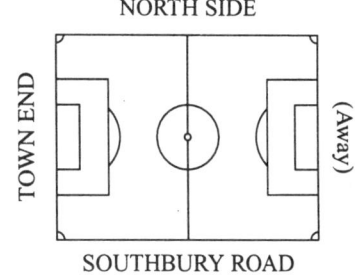

Travelling Supporters Information:
Routes: From North: Take M1 onto M25. Exit junction 25 onto A10 into Enfield; From South: Take A406
(North Circular) onto A10. Ground located at junction of A10 and A110.

GRAVESEND & NORTHFLEET FC

Founded: 1946
Former Name(s): Formed by Amalgamation of Gravesend United FC & Northfleet United FC
Nickname: 'The Fleet'
Ground: Stonebridge Road, Northfleet, Gravesend, Kent DA11 9BA
Record Attendance: 12,063 (1963)

Colours: Shirts - Red
    Shorts - White
Telephone No.: (01474) 533796
Contact No.: (01474) 363424
Pitch Size: 112 × 72yds
Ground Capacity: 3,300
Seating Capacity: 600

GENERAL INFORMATION
Supporters Club Administrator:
Terry Bobby
Address: c/o Club
Telephone Number: (01474) 533796
Car Parking: Car Park at Ground (450 cars)
Coach Parking: At Ground
Nearest Railway Station: Northfleet (5 mins)
Nearest Bus Station: Bus Stop outside ground (From Gravesend & Dartford)
Club Shop: At Ground
Opening Times: Matchdays Only
Telephone No.: (01474) 533796
Postal Sales: Yes, c/o Club
Nearest Police Station: Gravesend (3 miles)
Police Force: Gravesend
Police Telephone No.: (01474) 564346

GROUND INFORMATION
Away Supporters' Entrances: No Segregation
Away Supporters' Sections: No Segregation

DISABLED INFORMATION
Wheelchairs: 6 spaces available in total in Disabled Area – in front of Main Stand
Disabled Toilets: Available behind the Main Stand
Contact Nº: (01474) 533796

ADMISSION INFO (1997/98 PRICES)
Adult Standing: £5.00
Adult Seating: £5.50 or £6.50
Child Standing: £3.00
Child Seating: £3.50 or £4.00
Programme Price: £1.20
FAX Number: (01474) 323736

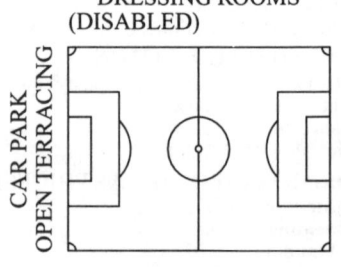

MAIN STAND (SEATING)
DRESSING ROOMS
(DISABLED)

CAR PARK
OPEN TERRACING

COVERED TERRACING

CLUBHOUSE
COVERED TERRACING

COVERED TERRACING

Travelling Supporters Information:
Routes: Take A2 to Northfleet/Southfleet exit along B262 to Northfleet then B2175 (Springhead Road) to the Junction with the A226. Turn left (The Hill, Northfleet) and follow road (Stonebridge Road). Ground is 1 mile on the right at foot of steep hill.

HARROW BOROUGH FC

Founded: 1933
Former Name(s): Roxonians FC, Harrow Town FC
Nickname: 'The Boro'
Ground: Earlsmead, Carlyon Avenue, South Harrow, Middlesex   HA2 8SS
Record Attendance: 3,000 v Wealdstone (1946)

Colours: Shirts - Red with White Trim
   Shorts - White
Telephone No.: (0181) 422-5221 (Office)
Daytime Phone No.: (0181) 422-5221
Pitch Size: 113 × 73yds
Ground Capacity: 3,068
Seating Capacity: 300

GENERAL INFORMATION
Supporters Club Administrator: R. Snook
Address: c/o Club
Telephone Number: (0181) 422-5221
Car Parking: Spaces for 120 Cars at Ground
Coach Parking: At Ground
Nearest Railway Station: Northolt Park (0.5 mile)
Nearest Tube Station: South Harrow LRT
Club Shop: Yes
Opening Times: Open every day with normal licensing hours
Telephone No.: (0181) 422-5221
Postal Sales: via Club
Nearest Police Station: South Harrow
Police Force: Metropolitan
Police Telephone No.: (0181) 900-7212

GROUND INFORMATION
Away Supporters' Entrances: Earlsmead
Away Supporters' Sections: Earlsmead

DISABLED INFORMATION
Wheelchairs: 8 spaces available in total in the Main Stand
Disabled Toilets: None
Contact Nº: (0181) 422-5221

ADMISSION INFO (1997/98 PRICES)
Adult Standing: £5.00
Adult Seating: £6.00
Child Standing: £2.50
Child Seating: £3.00
Programme Price: £1.00
FAX Number: (0181) 422-5221

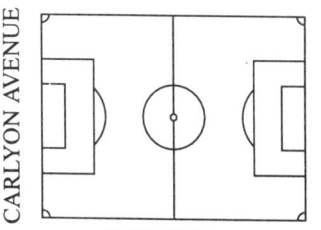

Travelling Supporters Information:
Routes: Exit M25 to M40 East, carry on to A40. Turn off at MacDonalds Northolt and travel past Northolt LRT station to Traffic Lights. Turn left to roundabout (near Eastcote Arms) then right into Eastcote Lane and right into Carlyon Avenue then finally right again into Earlsmead.

HENDON FC

GENERAL INFORMATION
Supporters Club Administrator:
Mike Hogan
Address: c/o Hendon FC
Telephone Number: (0181) 201-9494
Car Parking: Space for 200 Cars at Ground
Coach Parking: At Ground
Nearest Railway Station: Cricklewood (0.5 mile)
Nearest Tube Station: Brent Cross (0.5 mile)
Club Shop: Yes
Opening Times: Matchdays Only
Telephone No.: (0181) 201-9494
Postal Sales: Yes
Nearest Police Station: Golders Green
Police Force: Metropolitan
Police Telephone No.: (0181) 200-2212

GROUND INFORMATION
Away Supporters' Entrances: No Segregation
Away Supporters' Sections: –

DISABLED INFORMATION
Wheelchairs: 30 spaces available in total at the side of the Main Stand
Disabled Toilets: None
Contact Nº: (0181) 201-9494

ADMISSION INFO (1997/98 PRICES)
Adult Standing: £5.00
Adult Seating: £6.00
Child/Concessionary Standing: £3.00
Child/Concessionary Seating: £3.50
Programme Price: £1.20
FAX Number: (0181) 905-5966

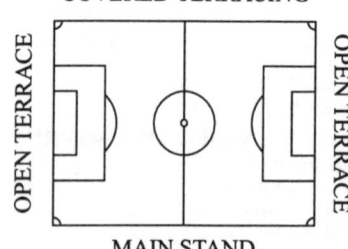

COVERED TERRACING
OPEN TERRACE
OPEN TERRACE
CAR PARK OPEN TERRACE
MAIN STAND
CLAREMONT ROAD

Travelling Supporters Information:
Routes: Take the M1 or North Circular Road to the southern end of the M1. At this intersection take the exit running parallel to the A406 on its eastern side (Tilling Road). Then take 2nd right past the Holiday Inn Hotel into Claremont Road and ground is on left.

HEYBRIDGE SWIFTS FC

Founded: 1882
Former Name(s): Heybridge F.C.
Nickname: 'The Swifts'
Ground: Scraley Road, Heybridge, Maldon, Essex   CM9 8JA
Record Attendance: 2,500 vs Woking
                      (1996/97)

Colours: Shirts - Black & White Stripes
            Shorts - Black
Telephone No.: (01621) 852978
Contact No.: (01621) 854798
Pitch Size: 110 × 72yds
Ground Capacity: 3,000
Seating Capacity: 550

GENERAL INFORMATION
Supporters Club Administrator: –
Address: c/o Social Club
Telephone Number: –
Car Parking: At ground
Coach Parking: At ground
Nearest Railway Station: Witham (6 miles)
Nearest Bus Station: Chelmsford
Club Shop: Yes
Opening Times: Matchdays Only
Telephone No.: C. Fenn (01621) 740878
Postal Sales: Yes
Nearest Police Station: Maldon
Police Force: Essex
Police Telephone No.: (01621) 852255

GROUND INFORMATION
Away Supporters' Entrances: No segregation
Away Supporters' Sections: No segregation

DISABLED INFORMATION
Wheelchairs: Accommodated
Disabled Toilets: Yes
Contact Nº: (01621) 854798

ADMISSION INFO (1997/98 PRICES)
Adult Standing: £5.00
Adult Seating: £5.00
Child/Concessionary Standing: £3.00
Child/Concessionary Seating: £3.00
Programme Price: £1.00
FAX Number: –

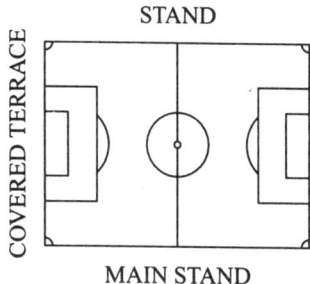

Travelling Supporters Information:
Routes: Take the A414 to Maldon then the B1026 towards Colchester and pass through Heybridge. Turn right at the sign for Tolleshunt Major (Scraley Road) and the ground is on the right.

HITCHIN TOWN FC

Founded: 1865 (re-formed 1928)
Former Name(s): Hitchin FC & Hitchin Blue
Cross FC
Nickname: 'The Canaries'
Ground: Top Field, Fishponds Road, Hitchin,
Herts   SG5 1NU
Record Attendance: 7,878 vs Wycombe
Wanderers (1956)

Colours: Shirts - Yellow
                  Shorts - Green
Telephone No.: (01462) 434483 (Club)
Daytime No.: (01462) 456003
Pitch Size: 114 × 78yds
Ground Capacity: 3,500
Seating Capacity: 400
Phone No.: (01462) 459028 (Matchdays only)

GENERAL INFORMATION
Supporters Club Administrator:
M. Williams
Address: 10 Karen House, Lower Stondon,
Bedfordshire
Telephone Number: (01462) 814226
Car Parking: Space for 150 cars at ground
Coach Parking: At Ground
Nearest Railway Station: Hitchin (1 mile)
Nearest Bus Station: Hitchin-Bancroft
Terminus (250 yards)
Club Shop: Yes
Opening Times: Matchdays Only
Phone No.: (0181) 883-2188 (Irvin Morgan)
Postal Sales: Yes
Nearest Police Station: Hitchin
Police Force: Hertfordshire
Police Telephone No.: (01438) 312323

GROUND INFORMATION
Away Supporters' Entrances: No Segregation
Away Supporters' Sections: No Segregation

DISABLED INFORMATION
Wheelchairs: 25 spaces in total available at the ends of
the Main Stand
Disabled Toilets: Available at rear of the Main Stand
Contact Nº: (01462) 434483

ADMISSION INFO (1997/98 PRICES)
Adult Standing: £5.00
Adult Seating: £5.00
Child Standing: £2.00
Child Seating: £ 2.00
Programme Price: £1.00
FAX Number: (01462) 482463

(BEDFORD ROAD)
MAIN STAND

FISHPONDS ROAD END
COVERED TERRACING

NEW ICKLEFORD
TERRACE

COVERED TERRACING
BEARTON ROAD

Travelling Supporters Information:
Routes: Take A1(M) to Junction 8 and follow A602 signposted to Hitchin. At Three Moorhens roundabout take 3rd exit onto A600 towards Bedford. At roundabout go straight over onto one way system, go straight over at the traffic lights, turn right at the next roundabout and the turnstiles are situated immediately on the left. Car Park turning 50 yards further on; Alternatively M1 to Junction 10: Follow well appointed signs to Hitchin via A505. On approach to Hitchen go straight over initial mini roundabout, turn left at next roundabout onto one way system, go straight over the traffic lights, turn right at the next roundabout and the turnstiles are situated immediately on the left. Car Park turning 50 yards further on; By Train: Hitchin Station is directly accessible via London Kings Cross, Finsbury Park, Stevenage, Cambridge, Huntingdon and Peterborough main line stations on Great Northern Line. 30 mins. from Kings Cross. From Hitchin Station turn right outside station approach follow around DIY store into Nightingale Road which leads down past Woolpack Pub to Victoria. Take Bunyan Road at The Victoria which leads into Fishponds Road.

KINGSTONIAN FC

Founded: 1885
Former Name(s): Kingston & Surbiton YMCA (1885-87); Saxons (1887-90); Kingston Wanderers (1890-93); Kingston on Thames (1893-1908); Old Kingstonians until 1919
Nickname: 'The K's'
Ground: Kingsmeadow Stadium, Kingston Road, Kingston upon Thames, Surrey KT1 3PB

Record Attendance: 4,582 vs Chelsea (1995)
Colours: Shirts - Red & White
 Shorts - Black
Telephone No.: (0181) 547-3335
Daytime Phone No.: (0181) 547-3335
Pitch Size: 115 × 80yds
Ground Capacity: 6,700
Seating Capacity: 700

GENERAL INFORMATION
Supporters Club Administrator: Ron Brown
Address: c/o Club
Telephone Number: (0181) 974-8717
Car Parking: Yes
Coach Parking: Yes
Nearest Railway Station: Norbiton (1 mile)
Nearest Bus Station: Kingston
Club Shop: Yes
Opening Times: 1.00-5.00pm & 7.00-9.00pm
Telephone No.: (0181) 547-3335
Postal Sales: Yes
Nearest Police Station: New Malden
Police Force: Metropolitan
Police Telephone No.: (0181) 541-1212

GROUND INFORMATION
Away Supporters' Entrances: No Segregation
Away Supporters' Sections: No Segregation

DISABLED INFORMATION
Wheelchairs: Accommodated around the ground
Disabled Toilets: Yes
Contact Nº: (0181) 547-3335

ADMISSION INFO (1997/98 PRICES)
Adult Standing: £5.00
Adult Seating: £6.00
Child Standing: £3.00
Child Seating: £4.00
Programme Price: £1.50
FAX Number: (0181) 947-5713

SMALL STAND

KINGSTON ROAD END

ATHLETICS END

MAIN STAND

Travelling Supporters Information:
Routes: Exit M25 at junction 10 and take the A3 to the New Malden/Worcester Park turn-off and turn into Malden Road (A2043). Follow Malden Road to the mini roundabout and turn left into Kingston Road. Kingsmeadow is situated approximately 1 mile up the Kingston Road, on the left-hand side and is sign-posted from the mini-roundabout.

OXFORD CITY FC

Founded: 1882	**Colours**: Shirts - White & Blue Hoops
Former Name(s): None	Shorts - White
Nickname: 'City'	**Telephone No.**: (01865) 744493 (Ground);
Ground: Court Place Farm, Marsh Lane,	(01865) 742394 (Club)
Marston, Oxford OX3 0NQ	**Contact No.**: (01865) 872181
Record Attendance: 9,500 vs Leytonstone	**Pitch Size**: 110 × 72yds
(Previous ground) (1950)	**Ground Capacity**: 3,000
	Seating Capacity: 300

GENERAL INFORMATION
Supporters Club Administrator: –
Address: c/o Clubhouse
Telephone Number: (01865) 742394
Car Parking: At Ground
Coach Parking: At Ground
Nearest Railway Station: Oxford
Nearest Bus Station: Oxford
Club Shop: None
Opening Times: –
Telephone No.: –
Postal Sales: –
Nearest Police Station: Cowley
Police Force: Thames Valley
Police Telephone No.: (01865) 749909

GROUND INFORMATION
Away Supporters' Entrances: No segregation
Away Supporters' Sections: No segregation

DISABLED INFORMATION
Wheelchairs: Accommodated
Disabled Toilets: Yes
Contact Nº: (01865) 872181

ADMISSION INFO (1997/98 PRICES)
Adult Standing: £5.00
Adult Seating: £5.00
Child Standing: £3.00
Child Seating: £3.00
Programme Price: £1.00
FAX Number: –

MAIN STAND

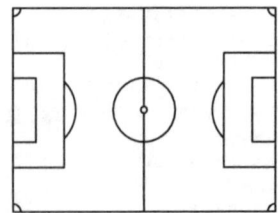

Travelling Supporters Information:
Routes: Exit M40 at junction 8 and take the A40 towards the City Centre. At Headington roundabout turn right along Northern bypass ring road and take first left at Marston flyover. Ground is on the left.

PURFLEET FC

Founded: 1985	**Colours**: Shirts - Yellow & Green
Former Name(s): None	Shorts - Green
Nickname: 'Fleet'	**Telephone No.**: (01708) 868901
Ground: Thurrock Hotel, Ship Lane, Grays,	**Contact No.**: (01708) 458301 (Match Sec)
Essex RM15 4HB	**Pitch Size**: 113 × 72yds
Record Attendance: 980 vs West Ham United	**Ground Capacity**: 3,500
(1989)	**Seating Capacity**: 300

GENERAL INFORMATION
Supporters Club Administrator: None
Address: –
Telephone Number: –
Car Parking: At Ground
Coach Parking: At Ground
Nearest Railway Station: Purfleet (2 miles)
Nearest Bus Station: Grays Town Centre
Club Shop: At Ground
Opening Times: Matchdays Only
Telephone No.: (01708) 868901
Postal Sales: –
Nearest Police Station: Grays
Police Force: Essex County Constabulary
Police Telephone No.: (01375) 391212

GROUND INFORMATION
Away Supporters' Entrances: No segregation
Away Supporters' Sections: –

DISABLED INFORMATION
Wheelchairs: No special area but accommodated
Disabled Toilets: Available in nearby Hotel
Contact Nº: (01708) 868901

ADMISSION INFO (1997/98 PRICES)
Adult Standing: £5.00
Adult Seating: £5.00
Child Standing: £2.50
Child Seating: £2.50
Programme Price: £1.00
FAX Number: (01708) 866703

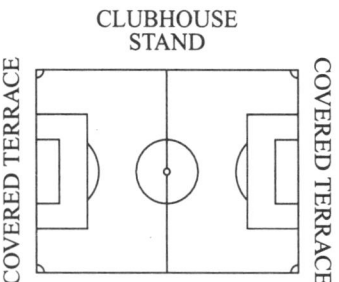

Travelling Supporters Information:
Routes: Take M25 or A13 to Dartford Tunnel roundabout – ground is then 50 yards on the right along Ship Lane.

ST. ALBANS CITY FC

Founded: 1908
Former Name(s): None
Nickname: 'The Saints'
Ground: Clarence Park, Hatfield Road,
St. Albans, Herts. AL1 4PL
Record Attendance: 9,757 vs Ferryhill Ath.
(27/2/26)

Colours: Shirts - Blue & Yellow
Shorts - Blue
Telephone No.: (01727) 866819 (Ground)
Daytime Phone No.: (01727) 864296 (Office)
Pitch Size: 110 × 80yds
Ground Capacity: 6,000
Seating Capacity: 900

GENERAL INFORMATION
Supporters Club Administrator:
Leigh Page
Address: 84 Ainsley Close, Edmonton,
London N9 9SH
Telephone Number: (0181) 365-3394
Car Parking: Street Parking
Coach Parking: In Clarence Park
Nearest Railway Station: St. Albans City
(200 yards)
Nearest Bus Station: City Centre (Short
Walk)
Club Shop: Yes
Opening Times: Matchdays Only
Telephone No.: (01727) 866819
Postal Sales: Contact: Leigh Page, as above
Nearest Police Station: Victoria Street,
St. Albans
Police Force: Hertfordshire
Police Telephone No.: (01707) 276122

GROUND INFORMATION
Away Supporters' Entrances: No Segregation
Away Supporters' Sections: –

DISABLED INFORMATION
Wheelchairs: 6 spaces each for home & away fans
accommodated in front of the Main Stand
Disabled Toilets: None
Contact Nº: (01727) 834920

ADMISSION INFO (1997/98 PRICES)
Adult Standing: £5.00
Adult Seating: £6.50
Child Standing: £3.00
Child Seating: £3.80
Programme Price: £1.30
FAX Number: None

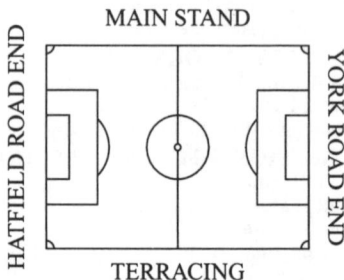

Travelling Supporters Information:
Routes: Take the M1 or M10 to the A405 North Orbital Road and at the roundabout at the start of the M10 go north on the A5183 (Watling Street). Turn right along St. Stephen's Hill and carry along into St. Albans. Continue up Holywell Hill go through two sets of traffic lights and at the end of St. Peter's Street take right turn at roundabout into Hatfield Road. Follow over mini-roundabouts and at second set of traffic lights turn left into Clarence Road, ground on left. Park in Clarence Road and enter ground via park or in York Road and use entrance by footbridge.

SUTTON UNITED FC

Founded: 1898
Former Name(s): Sutton Guild Rovers
Nickname: 'U's'
Ground: Borough Sports Ground, Gander Green Lane, Sutton, Surrey SM1 2EY
Record Attendance: 14,000 vs Leeds United (1970)

Colours: Shirts - Amber with Chocolate Trim
Shorts - Chocolate
Telephone No.: (0181) 644-4440
Daytime Phone No.: (0181) 644-4440
Pitch Size: 110 × 72yds
Ground Capacity: 6,652
Seating Capacity: 765

GENERAL INFORMATION
Supporters Club Administrator:
Tony Cove
Address: Flat 4, Overton Toft, 85 Mulgrave Road, Sutton, SM2 6CR
Telephone Number: (0181) 661-7918
Car Parking: 150 Cars behind Main Stand
Coach Parking: 1 Coach in Car Park
Nearest Railway Station: West Sutton Adj.
Nearest Bus Station: –
Club Shop: Yes
Opening Times: Matchdays Only
Telephone No.: –
Postal Sales: Yes
Nearest Police Station: Sutton
Police Force: Metropolitan
Police Telephone No.: (0181) 680-6212

GROUND INFORMATION
Away Supporters' Entrances: Collingwood Road
Away Supporters' Sections: Collingwood Road Terracing

DISABLED INFORMATION
Wheelchairs: 6 spaces each for home and away fans accommodated on the track perimeter
Disabled Toilets: 1 available alongside the Standing Terrace
Contact Nº: (0181) 644-4440

ADMISSION INFO (1997/98 PRICES)
Adult Standing: £5.00
Adult Seating: £6.00
Child Standing: £3.00
Child Seating: £3.50
Programme Price: £1.20
FAX Number: (0181) 644-5120

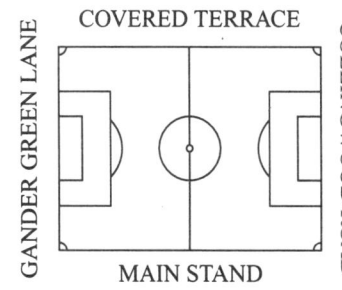

Travelling Supporters Information:
Routes: Exit M25 junction 8 (Reigate Hill) and travel North on A217 for approximately 8 miles. Cross A232 then turn right at next traffic lights (Gander PH) into Gander Green Lane. Ground 300 yards on left; From London: Gander Green Lane crosses Sutton Bypass 1 mile south of Rose Hill Roundabout. Avoid Sutton Town Centre especially on Saturdays.

WALTON & HERSHAM FC

Founded: 1886
Former Name(s): None
Nickname: 'The Swans'
Ground: Sports Ground, Stompond Lane,
Walton-On-Thames, Surrey   KT12 1HF
Pitch Size: 110 × 70yds
Record Attendance: 10,000 vs Crook Town

Colours: Shirts - Red & White
Shorts - White
Telephone No.: (01932) 244967
Contact Phone No.: (01932) 245263
Ground Capacity: 6,700
Seating Capacity: 500

GENERAL INFORMATION
Supporters Club Administrator: –
Address: c/o Club
Telephone Number: (01932) 245263
Car Parking: Spaces for 200 cars at Ground
Coach Parking: At Ground
Nearest Rail. Station: Walton-On-Thames
Nearest Bus Station: Kingston
Club Shop: Yes
Opening Times: Matchdays Only
Telephone No.: –
Postal Sales: Yes
Nearest Police Station: Walton-On-Thames
Police Force: Surrey
Police Telephone No.: –

GROUND INFORMATION
Away Supporters' Entrances: No usual segregation
Away Supporters' Sections: No usual segregation

DISABLED INFORMATION
Wheelchairs: Accommodated
Disabled Toilets: None
Contact N°: (01932) 245263

ADMISSION INFO (1997/98 PRICES)
Adult Standing: £5.00
Adult Seating: £6.00
Child Standing: £2.50
Child Seating: £3.00
Programme Price: £1.00
FAX Number: –

MAIN STAND

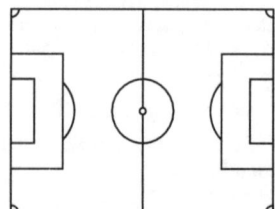

Travelling Supporters Information:
Routes: From M25: Leave at Junction 10 and take A3 to London. After short distance turn left onto A245 and at traffic lights turn right into Seven Hills Road. Proceed for approx 2 miles and at 2nd roundabout take 2nd exit. At next roundabout take 1st exit and at next roundabout the 3rd turn off into Stompond Lane. The car/coach park is approx 150m on right hand side; From A3: Leave at Junction with A245 and head towards Woking. At traffic lights proceed as above; From A244: Follow road over Walton Bridge and stay in middle lane at traffic lights. At the next lights stay in left hand lane and swing round to the right and go straight on. Stompond Lane is on the right after approximately 0.5 mile. A telephone kiosk is on the corner.

YEADING FC

Founded: 1965
Former Name(s): None
Nickname: 'The Ding'
Ground: The Warren, Beaconsfield Road, Hayes, Middlesex UB4 0SL
Record Attendance: 3,000 vs Hythe T. (1990)

Colours: Shirts - Red & Black Stripes
Shorts - Black
Telephone No.: (0181) 848-7362 (Social Club)
Daytime Phone No.: (0181) 848-7369 (Office)
Pitch Size: 115 × 72yds
Ground Capacity: 3,500
Seating Capacity: 250

GENERAL INFORMATION

Supporters Club Administrator:
David Lowe
Address: c/o Club
Telephone Number: (0181) 848-7369
Car Parking: Spaces for 200 cars at ground
Coach Parking: At Ground
Nearest Railway Station: Hayes (2 miles)
Nearest Bus Station: Uxbridge (2.5 miles)
Club Shop: Yes
Opening Times: Matchdays 1.30pm - 3.00pm
Weekdays 6.30pm – 7.30pm
Telephone No.: –
Postal Sales: Yes
Nearest Police Station: Uxbridge Road, Hayes
Police Force: Metropolitan
Police Telephone No.: (0181) 569-1212

GROUND INFORMATION

Away Supporters' Entrances: No Segregation
Away Supporters' Sections: No Segregation

DISABLED INFORMATION

Wheelchairs: No special facilities
Disabled Toilets: None
Contact Nº: (0181) 848-7362

ADMISSION INFO (1997/98 PRICES)

Adult Standing: £5.00
Adult Seating: £5.00
Child Standing: £3.00
Child Seating: £3.00
Programme Price: £1.00
FAX Number: (0181) 561-1063

COVERED TERRACING

SEATED STAND
CLUBHOUSE

Travelling Supporters Information:
Routes: Exit M4 junction 4 and A312 past Hayes & Harlington Station. Cross the Grand Union Canal and continue to Uxbridge Road crossroad. Turn right along Uxbridge Road toward Southall about 0.75 mile and turn right at the traffic lights into Springfield Road then left into Beaconsfield Road – ground is on the right at the bottom.
Note: Do not approach from Southall end of Beaconsfield Road as there is no access because of the Grand Union Canal!

ACCRINGTON STANLEY FC

Founded: 1876 (Reformed 1968)
Former Name(s): None
Nickname: 'Stanley' 'Reds'
Ground: Crown Ground, Livingstone Road, Accrington, Lancashire BB5 5BX
Record Attendance: 2,270 vs Gateshead (1992/93)

Colours: Shirts - Red
Shorts - White
Telephone No.: (01254) 383235
Daytime Phone No.: (01254) 383235
Pitch Size: 112 × 72yds
Ground Capacity: 4,000
Seating Capacity: 600

GENERAL INFORMATION
Supporters Club Administrator: Tony Clements
Address: 141 Manor Street, Accrington
Telephone Number: (01254) 393996
Car Parking: 250 Cars at Ground
Coach Parking: At Ground
Nearest Railway Station: Accrington (1.5 miles)
Nearest Bus Station: Accrington town centre
Club Shop: Yes
Opening Times: Daily
Telephone No.: (01254) 383235
Postal Sales: Yes
Nearest Police Station: Manchester Road, Accrington
Police Force: Lancashire County
Police Telephone No.: (01254) 382141

GROUND INFORMATION
Away Supporters' Entrances: Bottom Car Park
Away Supporters' Sections: Car Park Side

DISABLED INFORMATION
Wheelchairs: No specific areas but accommodated
Disabled Toilets: Yes
Contact Nº: (01254) 383235

ADMISSION INFO (1997/98 PRICES)
Adult Standing: £4.00
Adult Seating: £4.00
Child Standing: £2.00
Child Seating: £2.00
Programme Price: £1.00
FAX Number: (01254) 383235

CAR PARK

CAR PARK
ALTHAM END

DUCKWORTH STAND

Travelling Supporters Information:
Routes: Exit M66 onto A680 to Accrington. Travel through Town Centre, then turn right into Livingstone Road, approximately 500 yards past the Victoria Hospital.

ALFRETON TOWN FC

Founded: 1959	**Colours**: Shirts - Red & White
Former Name(s): None	Shorts - Red
Nickname: 'Reds'	**Telephone No.**: (01773) 830277
Ground: The Town Ground, North Street,	**Daytime Phone No.**: (01773) 832819 / 832413
Alfreton, Derbyshire	**Pitch Size**: 110 × 80yds
Record Attendance: 5,023 vs Matlock Town	**Ground Capacity**: 5,000
(1960)	**Seating Capacity**: 272

GENERAL INFORMATION
Supporters Club Administrator:
Dave Banks
Address: c/o Social Club
Telephone Number: –
Car Parking: At ground
Coach Parking: At ground
Nearest Railway Station: Alfreton (0.5 mile)
Nearest Bus Station: Alfreton
Club Shop: Yes
Opening Times: Matchdays and also open by appointment
Telephone No.: (01773) 836251
Postal Sales: Yes
Nearest Police Station: Hall Street, Alfreton
Police Force: Derbyshire
Police Telephone No.: –

GROUND INFORMATION
Away Supporters' Entrances: No segregation
Away Supporters' Sections: No segregation
DISABLED INFORMATION
Wheelchairs: Accommodated
Disabled Toilets: None
Contact Nº: (01773) 830277
ADMISSION INFO (1997/98 PRICES)
Adult Standing: £4.00
Adult Seating: £4.00
Child Standing: £2.00
Child Seating: £2.00
Programme Price: £1.00
FAX Number: c/o (01773) 832413

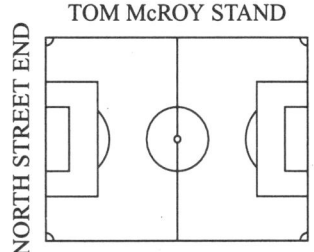

Travelling Supporters Information:
Routes: Exit M1 at junction 28 and take the A38 (signposted Derby). After 1 mile turn left onto the B600 then right at main road towards town centre. After 0.5 mile turn left down North Street. Ground is on right.

ALTRINCHAM FC

<table>
<tr><td>

Founded: 1903
Limited Company: 1921
Former Name(s): None
Nickname: 'The Robins'
Ground: Moss Lane, Altrincham, Greater Manchester WA15 8AP
Record Attendance: 10,275 (February 1925)

</td><td>

Colours: Shirts - Red and White Stripes
Shorts - Black
Telephone No.: (0161) 928-1045
Daytime Phone No.: (0161) 928-1045
Pitch Size: 115 × 70yds
Ground Capacity: 6,085
Seating Capacity: 1,154

</td></tr>
</table>

GENERAL INFORMATION
Supporters Club Administrator: P. Reid
Address: c/o Club
Telephone Number: –
Car Parking: Adjacent
Coach Parking: By Police Direction
Nearest Railway Station: Altrincham (5 minutes walk)
Nearest Bus Station: Altrincham
Club Shop:
Opening Times: Daily 9.00am to 5.00pm
Telephone No.: (0161) 928-1045
Postal Sales: Yes
Nearest Police Station: Dunham Road, Altrincham
Police Force: Greater Manchester
Police Telephone No.: (0161) 872-5050

GROUND INFORMATION
Away Supporters' Entrances: Chequers End Turn-stiles
Away Supporters' Sections: Chequers End of Ground

DISABLED INFORMATION
Wheelchairs: 3 spaces each for Home & Away fans adjacent to the Away dugout
Disabled Toilets: Yes
Contact Nº: (0161) 928-1045

ADMISSION INFO (1997/98 PRICES)
Adult Standing: £5.50
Adult Seating: £6.50
Child Standing: £3.50
Child Seating: £4.50
Programme Price: £1.20
FAX Number: (0161) 926-9934
Accompanied children under 14: £1.00

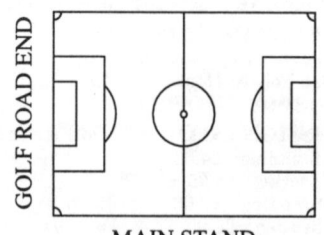

POPULAR SIDE
GOLF ROAD END
CHEQUERS END (Away)
MAIN STAND
MOSS LANE

Travelling Supporters Information:
Routes: Exit M56 junction 7 following signs Hale and Altrincham. Through 1st set of traffic lights and take 3rd right - Westminster Road and continue into Moss Lane. Ground on right.

BAMBER BRIDGE FC

Re-Founded: 1952	**Colours**: Shirts - White
Former Name(s): None	Shorts - Black
Nickname: 'The Brig'	**Contact Address**: Russ Rigby, c/o Club
Ground: Irongate, Brownedge Road, Bamber	**Contact Phone No.**: (01772) 909690
Bridge, Preston, Lancashire	**Pitch Size**: 110 × 78yds
Record Attendance: 2,241 v Preston NE (1988)	**Ground Capacity**: 2,600
Telephone No.: (01772) 627387	**Seating Capacity**: 250
Office No.: (01772) 909690	

GENERAL INFORMATION
Supporters Club Administrator: None
Address: –
Telephone Number: –
Car Parking: At Ground
Coach Parking: At Ground
Nearest Railway Station: Bamber Bridge (1.25 miles)
Nearest Bus Station: Bamber Bridge
Club Shop: Yes
Opening Times: Before & during matches
Telephone No.: –
Postal Sales: Yes – to ground address
Nearest Police Station: Bamber Bridge
Police Force: Lancashire Constabulary
Police Telephone No.: –

GROUND INFORMATION
Away Supporters' Entrances: No usual segregation
Away Supporters' Sections: No usual segregation

DISABLED INFORMATION
Wheelchairs: Accommodated
Disabled Toilets: Yes
Contact Nº: (01772) 909690

ADMISSION INFO (1997/98 PRICES)
Adult Standing: £4.00
Child Standing: £2.00
Programme Price: £1.00
FAX Number: (01772) 909691

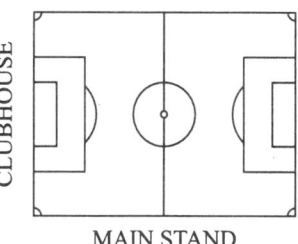

Travelling Supporters Information:
Routes: Exit M6 at junction 29 and follow Supermarket signs. Go straight through Traffic Lights and at 1st roundabout, bear right towards Preston onto London Way. The Ground is on the right as the road crosses the railway bridge and access is via the old course of Brownsedge Road, through the gates below the east side of the railway bridge.

BARROW AFC

Founded: 1901
Former Name(s): None
Nickname: 'Bluebirds'
Ground: Holker Street, Barrow-in-Furness, Cumbria
Record Attendance: 16,840 vs Swansea Town (1954)

Colours: Shirts - White
Shorts - Royal Blue
Telephone No.: (01229) 820346
Daytime Phone No.: (01229) 820346
Pitch Size: 110 × 75yds
Ground Capacity: 6,500
Seating Capacity: 1,264

GENERAL INFORMATION
Supporters Club Administrator: J. Smith
Address: c/o Club
Telephone Number: (01229) 826260
Car Parking: Street Parking, Popular Side Car Park and Soccer Bar Car Park
Coach Parking: Adjacent to Ground
Nearest Railway Station: Barrow Central (0.5 mile)
Nearest Bus Station: 0.5 mile
Club Shop: Yes
Opening Times: Monday to Friday 9.30am – 4.00pm
Telephone No.: (01229) 823061
Postal Sales: Yes
Nearest Police Station: Barrow
Police Force: Cumbria
Police Telephone No.: (01229) 824532

GROUND INFORMATION
Away Supporters' Entrances: –
Away Supporters' Sections: None Specified

DISABLED INFORMATION
Wheelchairs: 6 spaces available in the disabled bay
Disabled Toilets: Yes
Contact Nº: (01229) 820346

ADMISSION INFO (1997/98 PRICES)
Adult Standing: £4.00
Adult Seating: £5.50
Child Standing: £2.50
Child Seating: £3.00
Programme Price: £1.00
FAX Number: (01229) 820346
Social Club: (01229) 823061

```
          NEW STAND
   ┌─────────────────────────┐
 S │                         │ H
 M │                         │ O
 A │                         │ L
 L │    ┌───┐       ┌───┐    │ K
   │    │   │  ◯    │   │    │ E
 O │    └───┘       └───┘    │ R
 P │                         │
 E │                         │ S
 N │                         │ T
   │                         │ R
 E │                         │ E
 N │                         │ E
 D │                         │ T
   └─────────────────────────┘
          POPULAR END
```

Travelling Supporters Information:
Routes: Exit M6 junction 36 and take A590 through Ulverston. Turn right at the 1st roundabout on by-pass and follow signs for Barrow. After approximately 5 miles, the ground is on the left in Wilkie Road.

BISHOP AUCKLAND FC

Founded: 1886
Former Name(s): None
Nickname: 'The Bishops' 'The Blues'
Ground: Kingsway, Bishops Auckland,
Co. Durham   DL14 7JJ
Record Attendance: 17,000 vs Coventry City
(1952/53)

Colours: Shirts - Light & Dark Blue
Shorts - Navy
Telephone No.: (01388) 604403
Daytime Phone: (01388) 603686 (Social Club)
Pitch Size: 111 × 71yds
Ground Capacity: 5,500
Seating Capacity: 600

GENERAL INFORMATION
Supporters Club Administrator:
Tony Duffy
Address: 8 Ennerdale Grove, West Auckland
Co. Durham   DL14 9LN
Telephone Number: (01388) 833410
Car Parking: Yes at Ground
Coach Parking: In Town
Nearest Railway Station: Bishop Auckland
(0.5 mile)
Nearest Bus Station: Bishop Auckland
Club Shop: Yes
Opening Times: Matchdays Only
Telephone No.: (01388) 604403
Postal Sales: Yes
Nearest Police Station: Bishop Auckland
Police Force: County Durham
Police Telephone No.: (01388) 603566

GROUND INFORMATION
Away Supporters' Entrances: No usual segregation
Away Supporters' Sections: –

DISABLED INFORMATION
Wheelchairs: General location near pitch is available.
Disabled Toilets: None
Contact Nº: (01388) 604403

ADMISSION INFO (1997/98 PRICES)
Adult Standing: £4.00
Adult Seating: £4.50
Child Standing: £3.00
Child Seating: £4.00
Programme Price: £1.00
FAX Number: –

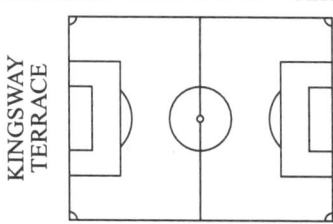

LIGHTFOOT   DELLWOOD
TERRACE   MAIN STAND   TERRACE

KINGSWAY TERRACE

CLUBHOUSE TERRACE
(COVERED)

Travelling Supporters Information:
Routes: From South: A1 to Scotch Corner then follow signs to Bishop Auckland, Ground behind Town Centre; From North & West: M6 to A66 at Tebay then A66 to Barnard Castle. Follow signs to Bishop Auckland, Ground behind Town Centre.

BLYTH SPARTANS FC

Founded: 1899
Former Name(s): None
Nickname: 'Spartans'
Ground: Croft Park, Blyth, Northumberland, NE24 3JE
Record Attendance: 10,186
Colours: Shirts - Green & White Stripes
Shorts - Green

Telephone No.: (01670) 352373 (Office)
Social Club: (01670) 354818
Contact Address: Stan Watson, 13 Benwell Grange, Benwell Lane, Newcastle-Upon-Tyne, NE15 6RG
Contact Phone No.: (0191) 273 9138
Pitch Size: 110 × 70yds
Ground Capacity: 6,000
Seating Capacity: 300

GENERAL INFORMATION
Supporters Club Administrator: Ronnie Clark
Address: c/o Club
Telephone Number: (01670) 353416
Car Parking: At Ground
Coach Parking: At Ground
Nearest Railway Station: Cramlington
Nearest Bus Station: Blyth (10 mins walk)
Club Shop: Yes
Opening Times: Matchdays Only
Telephone No.: –
Postal Sales: Yes
Nearest Police Station: Blyth
Police Force: Northumbria
Police Telephone No.: (01661) 872555

GROUND INFORMATION
Away Supporters' Entrances: No usual segregation
Away Supporters' Sections: No usual segregation

DISABLED INFORMATION
Wheelchairs: Accommodated
Disabled Toilets: Yes
Contact Nº: (01670) 361057

ADMISSION INFO (1997/98 PRICES)
Adult Standing: £4.00
Adult Seating: £4.50
Child Standing: £2.00
Child Seating: £2.50
Programme Price: £1.00
FAX Number: (01670) 352373

MAIN STAND

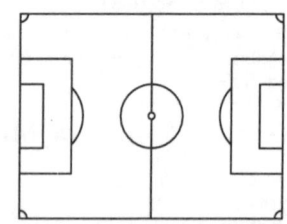

COVERED TERRACE & STAND

Travelling Supporters Information:
Routes: Pass through the Tyne Tunnel and take left lane for Morpeth (A19/A1). At the 2nd roundabout (approximately 7 miles) take full right turn for A189 (signposted Ashington). After 2 miles take slip road (A1061 signposted Blyth). Continue across 2 roundabouts and a railway crossing then turn left (A193) at next roundabout (signposted Blyth). Turn right for Quayside and ground is on left.

BOSTON UNITED FC

Founded: 1934	**Telephone No.**: (01205) 364406 (Office)
Former Name(s): Boston Town/Boston Swifts	**Daytime Phone No.**: (01205) 364406
Nickname: 'The Pilgrims'	**Matchday Phone No.**: (01205) 365525 or
Ground: York Street, Boston, Lincolnshire	365524
Record Attendance: 10,086 vs Corby Town	**Pitch Size**: - 112 × 72 yds
(1955)	**Ground Capacity**: 8,781
Colours: Shirts - Amber with Black Trim	**Seating Capacity**: 1,769
Shorts - Black	

GENERAL INFORMATION
Supporters Club Administrator: M.Fixter
Address: Browns Farm, Frampton, Boston, Lincs.
Telephone Number: (01205) 722182
Car Parking: At Ground
Coach Parking: At Ground
Nearest Railway Station: Boston (0.5 miles)
Nearest Bus Station: Boston Coach Station (0.25 mile)
Club Shop: 14/16 Spain Place, Boston
Opening Times: Weekdays 9.00am – 4.30pm; Saturdays 9.00am – 12.00pm & 6.00pm – 7.30pm
Telephone No.: (01205) 364406
Postal Sales: Yes
Nearest Police Station: Boston
Police Force: Lincolnshire
Police Telephone No.: (01205) 366222

GROUND INFORMATION
Away Supporters' Entrances: Town End
Away Supporters' Sections: Town End Enclosure

DISABLED INFORMATION
Wheelchairs: 5 spaces each for home & away fans accommodated at the York Street End
Disabled Toilets: None
Contact Nº: (01205) 364406

ADMISSION INFO (1997/98 PRICES)
Adult Standing: £4.00
Adult Seating: £4.50
Child Standing: £3.00
Child Seating: £3.50
Programme Price: £1.00
FAX Number: (01205) 354063

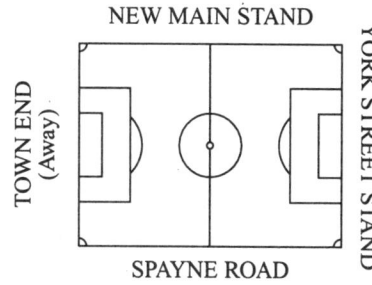

Travelling Supporters Information:
Routes: From North: Take A17 from Sleaford, bear right after railway crossing to traffic lights over bridge. Forward through traffic lights into York Street; From South & West: Take A16 from Spalding and turn right at traffic lights over bridge - forward through traffic lights into York Street.

CHORLEY FC

Founded: 1883	**Colours:** Shirts - Black & White Stripes
Former Name(s): None	Shorts - Black
Nickname: 'Magpies'	**Telephone No.:** (01257) 263406
Ground: Victory Park, Duke Street, Chorley,	**Daytime Phone No.:** (01257) 263406
PR7 3DU	**Pitch Size:** 112 × 72yds
Record Attendance: 9,679 v Darwen (1931/2)	**Ground Capacity:** 4,400
	Seating Capacity: 900

GENERAL INFORMATION
Supporters Club Administrator: –
Address: –
Telephone Number: –
Car Parking: 80 Cars at Ground
Coach Parking: At Ground
Nearest Railway Station: Chorley (0.25 ml)
Nearest Bus Station: 15 mins from Ground
Club Shop: Yes
Opening Times: 9.00am – 5.00pm weekdays
& matchdays
Telephone No.: (01257) 263406
Postal Sales: Yes
Nearest Police Station: St. Thomas's Road,
Chorley (10 minutes)
Police Force: Lancashire Constabulary
Police Telephone No.: (01257) 262831

GROUND INFORMATION
Away Supporters' Entrances: Ashby Street & Pilling
Lane Stands
Away Supporters' Sections: Pilling Lane Stand

DISABLED INFORMATION
Wheelchairs: Accommodated by arrangement
Disabled Toilets: None
Contact Nº: (01257) 263406

ADMISSION INFO (1997/98 PRICES)
Adult Standing: £4.00
Adult Seating: £5.00
Child Standing: £2.00
Child Seating: £2.50
Programme Price: £1.00

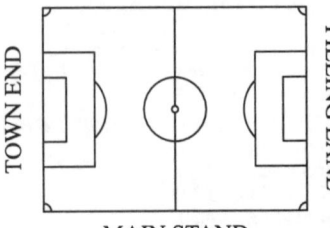

Travelling Supporters Information:
Routes: Exit M61 junction 6 and follow A6 to Chorley. Going past the Yarrow Bridge Hotel on Bolton Road, turn left at 1st set of lights into Pilling Lane. Take 1st right into Ashby Street, Ground 2nd entrance on left. Alternative Route: Exit M6 junction 27 and follow signs to Chorley. Turn left at lights and continue down the A49 for 2.5 miles before turning right onto B5251. On entering Chorley turn right into Duke Street 200 yards past The Plough.

COLWYN BAY FC

Founded: 1885
Former Name(s): None
Nickname: 'Bay' or 'Seagulls'
Ground: Llanelian Road, Old Colwyn, Clwyd
Correspondence Address: 15 Smith Avenue, Old Colwyn, Clwyd LL29 8BE
Record Attendance: 2,500

Colours: Shirts - Maroon/Dark Blue
Shorts - Maroon
Telephone No.: (01492) 516941
Daytime Phone No.: (01492) 515133
Pitch Size: 110 × 75yds
Ground Capacity: 2,500
Seating Capacity: 500

GENERAL INFORMATION
Supporters Club Administrator: A. Holden
Address: Flat 2, Erskine Road, Colwyn Bay, LL29 8EA
Telephone Number: (01492) 534287
Car Parking: At Ground
Coach Parking: At Ground
Nearest Railway Station: Colwyn Bay (1 ml)
Nearest Bus Station: Colwyn Bay
Club Shop: Yes at Ground
Opening Times: Matchdays only
Telephone No.: As for Supporters' Club
Postal Sales: Yes
Nearest Police Station: Colwyn Bay
Police Force: North Wales
Police Telephone No.: (01492) 517171

GROUND INFORMATION
Away Supporters' Entrances: No Segregation
Away Supporters' Sections: No Segregation

DISABLED INFORMATION
Wheelchairs: Accommodated in covered terrace
Disabled Toilets: Yes in Social Club
Contact Nº: (01492) 514581

ADMISSION INFO (1997/98 PRICES)
Adult Standing: £4.00
Adult Seating: £4.00
Child Standing: £2.00
Child Seating: £2.00
Programme Price: £1.00
FAX Number: (01492) 514581

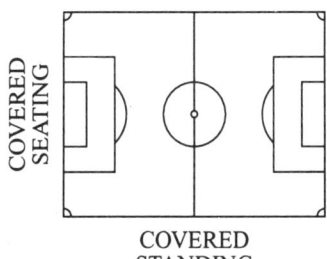

COVERED
STANDING

Travelling Supporters Information:
Routes: From Queensferry: Take A55 and when expressway is reached take the first exit off (signposted Old Colwyn). Turn left at the bottom of the slip road then straight on at mini roundabout into Llanelian Road. The ground is 0.5 mile on the right.

EMLEY FC

Founded: 1903
Former Name(s): None
Nickname: None
Ground: Emley Welfare Sports Ground,
Emley, Huddersfield, West Yorkshire
Record Attendance: 5,134 vs Barking (1/2/69)

Colours: Shirts - Maroon & Sky Blue
Shorts - Sky Blue
Telephone No.: (01924) 848398 (Social Club)
(01924) 840087 (Matchdays Only)
Daytime Phone No.: (01484) 860323 (Sec.)
Pitch Size: 110 × 70yds
Ground Capacity: 3,000
Seating Capacity: 220

GENERAL INFORMATION
Supporters Club Administrator: None
Address: –
Telephone Number: –
Car Parking: Spaces for 150 Cars at Ground
Coach Parking: At Ground
Nearest Railway Station: Huddersfield
(7 miles)
Nearest Bus Station: Huddersfield
Club Shop: Yes
Opening Times: Matchdays Only
Telephone No.: (01924) 848398
Postal Sales: Yes
Nearest Police Station: Kirkburton
Police Force: West Yorkshire
Police Telephone No.: (01484) 436897

GROUND INFORMATION
Away Supporters' Entrances: None Specified
Away Supporters' Sections: –

DISABLED INFORMATION
Wheelchairs: 3 spaces for home fans, 2 spaces for
away fans in front of the Main Stand
Disabled Toilets: One ladies and one gents under the
Main Stand
Contact Nº: (01924) 840087 or 848398

ADMISSION INFO (1997/98 PRICES)
Adult Standing: £4.00
Adult Seating: £4.50
Child Standing: £2.50
Child Seating: £3.00
Programme Price: £1.00
FAX Number: (01484) 851492

CRICKET GROUND SIDE

WARBURTON END

COVERED STANDING

THE ALEC HARDY STAND

Travelling Supporters Information:
Routes: Exit M1 junction 38 and follow signs to Huddersfield. Left at Roundabout onto Denby Dale Road
A636 for approximately 0.75 mile then turn right, 1 mile to Emley. From West: Exit M62 junction 23 and
follow road to Huddersfield. Take Ring Road out of Huddersfield following Wakefield signs for 5 miles,
through Lepton, past White Horse Public House on left, turn right at the top of the hill, Emley is 2.75 miles.

FRICKLEY ATHLETIC FC

Founded: 1910	**Colours**: Shirts - Blue
Former Name(s): Frickley Colliery FC	Shorts - Blue & White
Nickname: 'The Blues'	**Telephone No.**: (01977) 642460
Ground: Westfield Lane, South Emsell,	**Daytime Phone No.**: (01977) 643316
Pontefract, West Yorks.	**Pitch Size**: 117 × 78yds
Record Attendance: 6,500 vs Rotherham Utd.	**Ground Capacity**: 6,000
(1971)	**Seating Capacity**: 800

GENERAL INFORMATION
Supporters Club Administrator: –
Address: –
Telephone Number: –
Car Parking: 200 Cars at Ground
Coach Parking: At Ground
Nearest Railway Station: South Emsall (2 miles)
Nearest Bus Station: South Emsall
Club Shop: No
Opening Times: –
Telephone No.: –
Postal Sales: –
Nearest Police Station: South Kirkby
Police Force: West Yorkshire
Police Telephone No.: (01977) 793611

GROUND INFORMATION
Away Supporters' Entrances: No Segregation
Away Supporters' Sections: –

DISABLED INFORMATION
Wheelchairs: Accommodated within perimeter wall
Disabled Toilets: Available in the Stand
Contact Nº: (01977) 643316

ADMISSION INFO (1997/98 PRICES)
Adult Standing: £4.00
Adult Seating: £5.00
Child Standing: £2.00
Child Seating: £3.00
Programme Price: £1.00
FAX Number: (01977) 642460

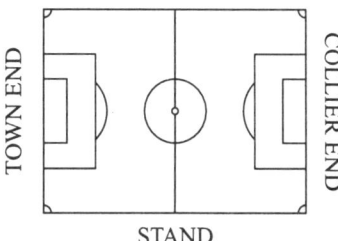

TOWN END

COLLIER END

STAND

Travelling Supporters Information:
Routes: From North: Follow A1 south leave A1 at first exit after Trusthouse Forte TraveLodge and follow road to South Kirkby then onto South Emsall. Upon entering the Town Centre take Westfield Lane then Oxford Street; From South: Take M1 to M18 to A1(M) and finally onto A638. Follow road towards Wakefield then follow road to South Emsall, then as above; From West & East: Take M62 to junction with A1 and head south to first exit, then as North.

GAINSBOROUGH TRINITY FC

Founded: 1873
Former Name(s): None
Nickname: 'The Blues'
Ground: The Northolme, North Street, Gainsborough, Lincolnshire
Record Attendance: 9,760 vs Scunthorpe Utd. (1948)

Colours: Shirts - Blue
Shorts - White
Telephone No.: (01427) 613295 (Office)
Clubhouse No.: (01427) 615625
Daytime Phone No.: (01427) 612333
Pitch Size: 111 × 71yds
Ground Capacity: 3,500
Seating Capacity: 228

GENERAL INFORMATION
Supporters Club Administrator: P. Oxby
Address: c/o Club
Telephone Number: (01427) 613688
Car Parking: Street Parking
Coach Parking: Opposite Ground
Nearest Railway Station: Lea Road (2 miles)
Nearest Bus Station: Heaton Street (1 mile)
Club Shop: Yes
Opening Times: Matchdays Only
Telephone No.: (01427) 613295
Postal Sales: Yes
Nearest Police Station: Morton Terrace (0.5 mile)
Police Force: Lincolnshire
Police Telephone No.: (01427) 810910

GROUND INFORMATION
Away Supporters' Entrances: No Segregation
Away Supporters' Sections: –

DISABLED INFORMATION
Wheelchairs: No specified area but accommodated
Disabled Toilets: None
Contact Nº: (01427) 615625 or 613295

ADMISSION INFO (1997/98 PRICES)
Adult Standing: £4.00
Adult Seating: £4.50
Child Standing: £2.00
Child Seating: £2.50
Programme Price: £1.00
FAX Number: (01427) 613295

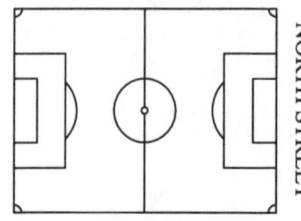

CARLISLE STREET

NORTH STREET

NORTHOLME

Travelling Supporters Information:
Routes: From North, South & West: Exit A1 near Worksop on to the A614 and take first left onto the B6420 to East Retford. Turn right on to A620 to Gainsborough and after 12 miles on outskirts of town take A631. Cross bridge, passing church and turn left along the A159. Pass Post Office and ground is 300 yards along North Street; From East: Take A631 into Gainsborough and turn left on to A159 then as North.

GUISELEY AFC

Founded: 1909	**Colours**: Shirts - White with Blue Sleeves
Former Name(s): None	Shorts - Blue
Nickname: None	**Telephone No.**: (01943) 873223
Ground: Nethermoor, Otley Road, Guiseley,	**Social Club No.**: (01943) 872872
Leeds, LS20 8BT	**Pitch Size**: 110 × 69yds
Record Attendance: 2,486 v Bridlington Town	**Ground Capacity**: 3,000
(1989/90)	**Seating Capacity**: 427

GENERAL INFORMATION
Supporters Club Administrator:
Les Wood
Address: c/o Club
Telephone Number: (0113) 250-9181
Car Parking: At ground & Ings Crescent
Coach Parking: At Ground
Nearest Railway Station: Guiseley (5 minute walk)
Nearest Bus Station: Bus Stop outside Ground
Club Shop: Yes
Opening Times: Matchdays Only
Telephone No.: (01943) 873223
Postal Sales: Yes
Nearest Police Station: Otley
Police Force: West Yorkshire
Police Telephone No.: (01532) 585065

GROUND INFORMATION
Away Supporters' Entrances: No segregation
Away Supporters' Sections: No segregation

DISABLED INFORMATION
Wheelchairs: Accommodated by Players' Entrance
Disabled Toilets: None
Contact Nº: (01943) 879236

ADMISSION INFO (1997/98 PRICES)
Adult Standing: £4.00
Adult Seating: £4.00
Child Standing: £2.00
Child Seating: £2.00
Programme Price: £1.00
FAX Number: (01943) 873223

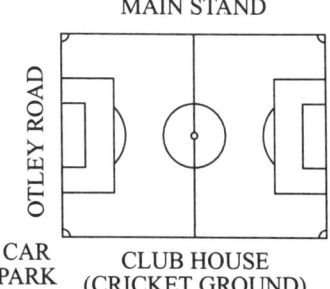

Travelling Supporters Information:
Routes: Exit M62 Junction 28 and take Leeds Road to Roundabout at Junction of A65 at Horsforth. Turn left onto A65 pass through Rawdon to Guiseley. Ground is 0.25 mile on right after traffic lights opposite Silver Cross factory.

HYDE UNITED FC

Founded: 1919	**Colours**: Shirts - Red
Former Name(s): Hyde FC (1885-1917)	Shorts - Black
Nickname: 'Tigers'	**Telephone No.**: (0161) 368-1031 (Matchdays)
Ground: Tameside Stadium, Ewen Fields,	**Daytime Phone No.**: (0161) 368-3687
Walker Lane, Hyde, Cheshire SK14 2SB	**Pitch Size**: 120 × 70yds
Record Attendance: 9,500 vs Nelson (1952)	**Ground Capacity**: 4,000
	Seating Capacity: 400

GENERAL INFORMATION
Supporters Club Administrator:
Mark Dring
Address: 16 Gainsborough Walk, Denton,
Manchester
Telephone Number: (0161) 336-8076
Car Parking: 150 Cars at ground
Coach Parking: At Ground
Nearest Railway Station: Newton (0.25 ml)
Nearest Bus Station: Hyde
Club Shop: Yes
Opening Times: Matchdays Only
Telephone No.: (0161) 368-1031 or 368-3687
Postal Sales: Yes
Nearest Police Station: Hyde
Police Force: Tameside Area
Police Telephone No.: (0161) 330-8321

GROUND INFORMATION
Away Supporters' Entrances: None Specified
Away Supporters' Sections: –

DISABLED INFORMATION
Wheelchairs: No specific area but accommodated
Disabled Toilets: Yes
Contact Nº: (0161) 368-3687

ADMISSION INFO (1997/98 PRICES)
Adult Standing: £5.00
Adult Seating: £6.00
Child Standing: £3.00
Child Seating: £4.00
Programme Price: £1.00
FAX Number: (0161) 368-3687 (Secretary);
(0161) 368-1031 (Ground)

MAIN STAND

TINKERS PASSAGE

WALKER LANE

LEIGH STREET SCHOOL

Travelling Supporters Information:
Routes: On entering Hyde follow signs for Tameside Leisure Park. When on Walker Lane, take 2nd Car Park entrance near Leisure Pool and follow road round for Stadium.

KNOWSLEY UNITED FC

Founded: 1983	**Colours**: Shirts - Red + Black Hoops
Former Name(s): Kirkby Town FC	Shorts - Black
Nickname: 'United'	**Telephone No.**: (0151) 480-2529 (Social Club)
Ground: Alt Park, Endmoor Road, Huyton,	**Ground No.**: (0151) 480-8077
Liverpool, L36	**Pitch Size**: 112 × 75yds
Record Attendance: 951 vs Stafford Rangers	**Ground Capacity**: 3,500
(1993 F.A. Cup)	**Seating Capacity**: 350

GENERAL INFORMATION
Supporters Club Administrator: None
Address: –
Telephone Number: –
Car Parking: At Ground
Coach Parking: At Ground
Nearest Railway Station: Huyton (3 miles)
Club Shop: None at Present
Opening Times: –
Telephone No.: –
Postal Sales: –
Nearest Police Station: Huyton (3 miles)
Police Force: Merseyside
Police Telephone No.: –

GROUND INFORMATION
Away Supporters' Entrances: No segregation
Away Supporters' Sections: No segregation

DISABLED INFORMATION
Wheelchairs: 4 spaces each for home and away fans
Disabled Toilets: Two available inside the complex
Contact Nº: (0151) 480-2529

ADMISSION INFO (1997/98 PRICES)
Adult Standing: £4.00
Adult Seating: £4.00
Child Standing: £2.00
Child Seating: £2.00
Programme Price: £1.00
FAX Number: (0151) 480-8077

MAIN STAND

CLUBHOUSE

(TRAINING PITCH) OPEN TERRACING

OPEN TERRACING

Travelling Supporters Information:
Routes: Exit M62 junction 6 and take M57 to junction 3. Follow signs for Huyton and at roundabout go straight across along Huyton Link Road. Ground is on left.

LANCASTER CITY FC

Founded: 1902
Former Name(s): Lancaster Town FC
Nickname: 'Dolly Blues'
Ground: Giant Axe, West Road, Lancaster, LA1 5PE
Record Attendance: 7,500 vs Carlisle United (1936)

Colours: Shirts - Blue
         Shorts - White
Telephone No.: (01524) 382238
Ground No.: (01524) 841950
Pitch Size: 112 × 72yds
Ground Capacity: 5,000
Seating Capacity: 450

GENERAL INFORMATION
Supporters Club Administrator: None
Address: –
Telephone Number: –
Car Parking: At Ground
Coach Parking: At Ground
Nearest Railway Station: Lancaster (5 mins. walk)
Nearest Bus Station: Lancaster (5 minutes)
Club Shop: Yes
Opening Times: Matchdays
Telephone No.: (01524) 382238
Postal Sales: –
Nearest Police Station: Lancaster
Police Force: Lancashire
Police Telephone No.: (01524) 63333

GROUND INFORMATION
Away Supporters' Entrances: No segregation
Away Supporters' Sections: No segregation

DISABLED INFORMATION
Wheelchairs: Accommodated
Disabled Toilets: –
Contact Nº: (01524) 35774

ADMISSION INFO (1997/98 PRICES)
Adult Standing: £4.00
Adult Seating: £4.00
Child Standing: £2.00
Child Seating: £2.00
Programme Price: £1.00
FAX Number: (01524) 382238

MAIN STAND

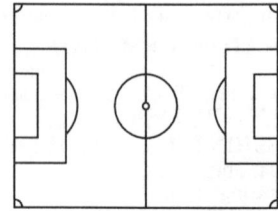

COVERED TERRACE

Travelling Supporters Information:
Routes: From the South: Exit M6 at junction 33 and follow road into City. Turn left at the traffic lights after Waterstones Bookshop then take the second right passing railway station on the right. Follow road down hill and the ground is 1st right; From the North: Exit M6 at junction 34 and bear left onto A683. Go into one-way system in the City and pass Police Station. At the next traffic lights by Alexandra pub, follow road back into centre then as from South.

LEIGH RMI FC

Founded: 1896
Former Name(s): Horwich RMI FC
Nickname: 'The Railwaymen'
Ground: Hilton Park, Kirkhall Lane, Leigh, WN7 1RN
Record Attendance: Not Known

Colours: Shirts - Red &White Stripes
Shorts - Black With Red Trim
Telephone No.: (01942) 743743
Pitch Size: 112 × 75yds
Ground Capacity: 9,240
Seating Capacity: 1,425

GENERAL INFORMATION
Supporters Club Administrator: Neil Smith
Address: c/o Club
Telephone Number: (01942) 743743
Car Parking: Spaces for 150 cars at Ground
Coach Parking: At Ground
Nearest Railway Station: Atherton
Nearest Bus Station: Leigh
Club Shop: No
Opening Times: –
Telephone No.: –
Postal Sales: –
Nearest Police Station: Leigh
Police Force: Lancs
Police Telephone No.: (01942) 244981

GROUND INFORMATION
Away Supporters' Entrances: No Segregation
Away Supporters' Sections: –

DISABLED INFORMATION
Wheelchairs: Accommodated by arrangement
Disabled Toilets: No
Contact Nº: (01942) 743743

ADMISSION INFO (1997/98 PRICES)
Adult Standing: £4.00
Adult Seating: £4.00
Child Standing: £1.00 (or free with adult)
Child Seating: £1.00 (or free with adult)
Programme Price: £1.00
FAX Number: –

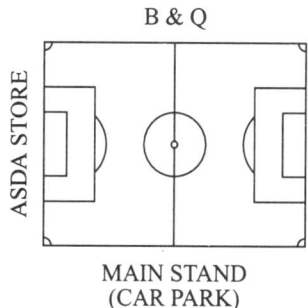

Travelling Supporters Information:
Routes: Come off M61 at Junction 5 (Westhoughton, Bolton), follow the Westhoughton sign to roundabout then pick up the Leigh sign. Keep on the main road to the traffic lights, turn left onto Leigh Road and carry on about 3 miles to the traffic lights. Turn left and 1st right to the next set of traffic lights. Turn right onto Atheleigh Way, A579 at the 1st set of traffic lights, turn left (B & Q on right), at the next set of traffic lights. Turn right (Leigh Town Centre), at the second opening on the right turn into Prescott Street, carry on to the top, turn right, ground to the left.

MARINE FC

Founded: 1894
Former Name(s): None
Nickname: 'Mariners' 'Lilywhites'
Ground: Rossett Park, College Road, Crosby, Liverpool L23 3AS
Record Attendance: 4,000 vs Nigeria (1949)

Colours: Shirts - White
Shorts - Black
Telephone No.: (0151) 924-1743 (Office)
Daytime Phone: (0151) 924-4046 (Clubhouse)
Pitch Size: 112 × 71yds
Ground Capacity: 2,500
Seating Capacity: 400

GENERAL INFORMATION
Supporters Club Administrator:
Mark Prescott
Address: 5 Vale Lodge, Rice Lane, Walton, Liverpool L9 1LR
Telephone Number: (0151) 524-1608
Car Parking: 60 Cars at Ground
Coach Parking: –
Nearest Railway Station: Blundellsands & Crosby (800 yards)
Nearest Bus Station: Crosby
Club Shop: Yes
Opening Times: Matchdays Only
Telephone No.: (0151) 523-1608
Postal Sales: Yes
Nearest Police Station: Crosby
Police Force: Merseyside
Police Telephone No.: (0151) 709-6010

GROUND INFORMATION
Away Supporters' Entrances: Gate A
Away Supporters' Sections: –

DISABLED INFORMATION
Wheelchairs: Accommodated in front of the Stand
Disabled Toilets: None
Contact Nº: (0151) 924-1743

ADMISSION INFO (1997/98 PRICES)
Adult Standing: £4.00
Adult Seating: £4.50
Child Standing: £2.50
Child Seating: £3.00
Programme Price: £1.00
FAX Number: (0151) 924-1743

ROSSETT ROAD
(Closed to Spectators)

CROSSENDER STAND

COLLEGE ROAD CLUB END

JUBILEE ROAD
COVERED

Travelling Supporters Information:
Routes: Follow M57/M58 Motorway to end. Follow signs into Crosby Town Centre, ground is situated on College Road which is off main Liverpool-Southport A565 road. Ground is sign-posted in town.

RADCLIFFE BOROUGH FC

Founded: 1949	**Colours**: Shirts - Blue
Former Name(s): None	Shorts - Blue
Nickname: 'Boro'	**Telephone No.**: (0161) 724-8363 (Office)
Ground: Stainton Park, Pilkington Road,	**Clubhouse No.**: (0161) 724-5937
Radcliffe, Manchester M26 0PE	**Pitch Size**: 115 × 75yds
Record Attendance: 1,365 vs Caernarfon	**Ground Capacity**: 3,000
Town (1983)	**Seating Capacity**: 450

GENERAL INFORMATION
Supporters Club Administrator: None
Address: –
Telephone Number: –
Car Parking: At Ground
Coach Parking: At Ground
Nearest Railway Station: Radcliffe (1 mile)
Nearest Bus Station: Radcliffe
Club Shop: None
Opening Times: –
Telephone No.: –
Postal Sales: –
Nearest Police Station: Radcliffe
Police Force: Greater Manchester
Police Telephone No.: (0161) 856-8296

GROUND INFORMATION
Away Supporters' Entrances: No segregation
Away Supporters' Sections: No segregation

DISABLED INFORMATION
Wheelchairs: Accommodated
Disabled Toilets: None
Contact Nº: (0161) 724-8363

ADMISSION INFO (1997/98 PRICES)
Adult Standing: £4.00
Adult Seating: £4.00
Child Standing: £2.00
Child Seating: £2.00
Programme Price: 70p
FAX Number: (0161) 723-3178

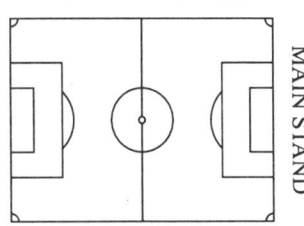

COVERED TERRACING

MAIN STAND

OPEN TERRACING

Travelling Supporters Information:
Routes: Exit M6 junction 17 and follow signs for Whitefield & Bury. Take the A665 to Radcliffe via by-pass to Bolton Road. Turn right into Unsworth Street opposite Turf Hotel. After about 0.5 mile turn left into Colshaw Close East for Ground.

RUNCORN FC

<table>
<tr><td>

Founded: 1919
Former Name(s): None
Nickname: 'The Linnets'
Ground: Canal Street, Runcorn, Cheshire
Record Attendance: 10,111 vs Preston N.E.
(1938/39)

</td><td>

Colours: Shirts - Yellow
Shorts - Green
Telephone No.: (01928) 575858 (Social Club)
Daytime Phone No.: (01928) 560076
Pitch Size: 110 × 70yds
Ground Capacity: 4,500
Seating Capacity: 449

</td></tr>
</table>

GENERAL INFORMATION
Supporters Club Administrator: Noel Bell
Address: c/o Club
Telephone Number: (01928) 560076
Car Parking: At Ground
Coach Parking: At Ground
Nearest Railway Station: Runcorn (1 mile)
Nearest Bus Station: Runcorn Old Town
(1 mile)
Club Shop:Yes
Opening Times: Matchdays Only
Telephone No.: None
Postal Sales: Yes
Nearest Police Station: Shopping City,
Runcorn
Police Force: Cheshire
Police Telephone No.: (01928) 713456

GROUND INFORMATION
Away Supporters' Entrances: River End
Away Supporters' Sections: River End

DISABLED INFORMATION
Wheelchairs: No specific area but accommodated
Disabled Toilets: 2 available inside the Social Club
Contact Nº: (01928) 560076

ADMISSION INFO (1997/98 PRICES)
Adult Standing: £5.00
Adult Seating: £6.00
Child Standing: £2.50
Child Seating: £3.00
Programme Price: £1.20
FAX Number: (01928) 560076

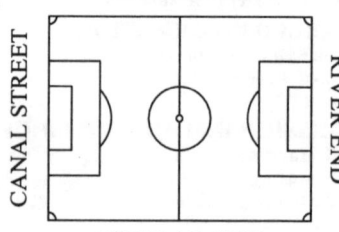

MAIN STAND

CANAL STREET

RIVER END

POPULAR SIDE

Travelling Supporters Information:
Routes: Exit M56 junction 11 and follow signs for Runcorn Old Town.
Or: Exit M62 at junction 7 and take the road to Widnes (following signs for Runcorn & Widnes Bridge).
Cross over bridge and follow signs for Runcorn Old Town then take 2nd exit for ground.

SPENNYMOOR UNITED FC

Founded: 1901	**Colours**: Shirts - Black & White Stripes
Former Name(s): None	Shorts - Black
Nickname: 'The Moors'	**Telephone No.**: (01388) 811934
Ground: Brewery Field, Durham Road,	**Daytime Phone No.**: (01388) 814100
Spennymoor, Co. Durham, DL16 6JN	**Pitch Size**: 113 × 70yds
Record Attendance: 7,202 v Bishop Auckland	**Ground Capacity**: 5,000
(30/3/57)	**Seating Capacity**: 300

GENERAL INFORMATION
Supporters Club Administrator:
David Graves
Address: c/o Club
Telephone Number: (01388) 811934
Car Parking: Street Parking
Coach Parking: Club will arrange
Nearest Railway Station: Durham (6 miles)
Nearest Bus Station: Durham (6 miles)
Club Shop: Yes
Opening Times: Matchdays Only
Telephone No.: –
Postal Sales: Yes
Nearest Police Station: Spennymoor
Police Force: Durham Constabulary
Police Telephone No.: (01388)

GROUND INFORMATION
Away Supporters' Entrances: No segregation
Away Supporters' Sections: No segregation

DISABLED INFORMATION
Wheelchairs: Accommodated by arrangement
Disabled Toilets: Available in Clubhouse
Contact Nº: (01388) 811934

ADMISSION INFO (1997/98 PRICES)
Adult Standing: £4.00
Adult Seating: £4.50
Child Standing: £2.00
Child Seating: £2.50
Programme Price: £1.00
FAX Number: (01388) 811934

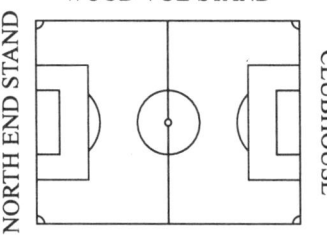

Travelling Supporters Information:
Routes: From South: Take A1(M) to A167 then A688. On entering Spennymoor go straight across mini-roundabout then take 3rd exit at next roundabout (by St. Andrew's Church). Pass Asda on left and continue straight on at junction passing Salvin Arms. Ground then 200 yards on left. From North: Take A167 to Croxdale (Ness factory) turn right at cemetery into Durham Road. Ground 0.5 mile on the right.

WINSFORD UNITED FC

Founded: 1883
Former Name(s): Over Wanderers FC (prior to 1914)
Nickname: 'Blues'
Ground: Barton Stadium, Wharton, Winsford, Cheshire CW7 3EU
Record Attendance: 7,000 vs Witton Albion (1947)

Colours: Shirts - Royal Blue
Shorts - White
Telephone No.: (01606) 593021
Contact No.: (01606) 554295 (Secretary)
Daytime Phone: (01606) 861980 (Social Club)
Pitch Size: 112 × 75yds
Ground Capacity: 3,000
Seating Capacity: 250

GENERAL INFORMATION
Supporters Club Administrator: –
Address: c/o Club
Telephone Number: –
Car Parking: Space for 200 cars at ground
Coach Parking: At ground
Nearest Railway Station: Winsford (1 mile)
Nearest Bus Station: Northwich
Club Shop: Yes
Opening Times: Matchdays Only
Telephone No.: (01606) 593021
Postal Sales: Yes
Nearest Police Station: Winsford
Police Force: Cheshire
Police Telephone No.: (01606) 592222

GROUND INFORMATION
Away Supporters' Entrances: No usual segregation
Away Supporters' Sections: Big games only

DISABLED INFORMATION
Wheelchairs: Accommodated beside the Main Stand
Disabled Toilets: Yes
Contact Nº: (01606) 861980

ADMISSION INFO (1997/98PRICES)
Adult Standing: £4.50
Adult Seating: £4.50
Child Standing: £2.50
Child Seating: £2.50
Programme Price: £1.00
FAX Number: (01606) 593021

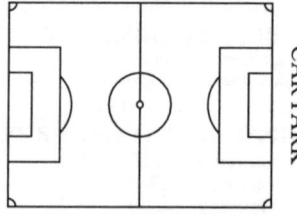

KINGSWAY

CAR PARK

WHARTON REC.

Travelling Supporters Information:
Routes: From North: Exit M6 at junction 19 and take A556 towards Northwich and Davenham, then follow A5018 to Winsford; From South: Exit M6 at junction 18 and follow A54 through Middlewich to Winsford. Turn off main road opposite lakeside park into Wharton Road and bear left. Ground is 0.25 mile along on the right.

ATHERSTONE UNITED FC

Founded: 1979
Former Name(s): None
Nickname: 'The Adders'
Ground: Sheepy Road, Atherstone, Warwickshire
Office Address: 18 Greendale Close, Atherstone, Warks. CV9 1PR
Record Attendance: 2,873 vs V.S. Rugby FC (1987/88)

Colours: Shirts - Red & White Stripes
Shorts - Red
Telephone No.: (01827) 717829
Daytime Phone No.: (01827) 714326
Pitch Size: 115 × 80yds
Ground Capacity: 3,500
Seating Capacity: 353

GENERAL INFORMATION
Supporters Club Administrator: S. Gilbert
Address: 7 River Drive, Atherstone, Warks. CV9 3SR
Telephone Number: –
Car Parking: Adjacent to Ground
Coach Parking: Adjacent to Ground
Nearest Railway Station: Atherstone (1 ml)
Nearest Bus Station: Atherstone/Nuneaton
Club Shop: At Ground
Opening Times: Matchdays Only
Telephone No.: (01827) 717829
Postal Sales: –
Nearest Police Station: Atherstone 200 yards
Police Force: Warwicks
Police Telephone No.: (01827) 718092

GROUND INFORMATION
Away Supporters' Entrances: Gipsy Lane
Away Supporters' Sections: Gipsy Lane

DISABLED INFORMATION
Wheelchairs: 4 spaces available in the Centre Stand
Disabled Toilets: None
Contact Nº: (01827) 714326

ADMISSION INFO (1997/98 PRICES)
Adult Standing: £5.00
Adult Seating: £5.00
Child Standing: £2.50
Child Seating: £2.50
Programme Price: £1.00
FAX Number: (01203) 349989
Note: UB-40's – concessionary prices

MAIN STAND

OPEN TERRACE

OPEN TERRACE

COVERED TERRACE

Travelling Supporters Information:
Routes: Take A5 into Town. Follow directions for Twycross Sheepy Magna – ground 0.5 mile on left.

BATH CITY FC

Founded: 1889	**Colours**: Shirts - Black & White Stripes
Former Name(s): None	Shorts - Black
Nickname: 'City' or 'Romans'	**Telephone No.**: (01225) 423087
Ground: Twerton Park, Bath BA2 1DB	**Daytime Phone No.**: (01225) 423087
Record Attendance: 18,020 vs Brighton &	**Pitch Size**: 110 × 76yds
Hove Albion (1960)	**Ground Capacity**: 8,840
	Seating Capacity: 1,026

GENERAL INFORMATION
Supporters Club Administrator:
Mr. J. Turner
Address: c/o Club
Telephone Number: (01225) 313247
Car Parking: 150 spaces at Ground
Coach Parking: Avon Street, Bath
Nearest Railway Station: Bath Spa
(1.5 miles)
Nearest Bus Station: Avon Street, Bath
Club Shop: Yes
Opening Times: Matchdays Only
Telephone No.: (01225) 423087
Postal Sales: Yes
Nearest Police Station: Bath (1.5 miles)
Police Force: Avon & Somerset
Police Telephone No.: (01225) 842439

GROUND INFORMATION
Away Supporters' Entrances: Bristol End
Away Supporters' Sections: Bristol End

DISABLED INFORMATION
Wheelchairs: 10 spaces each for Home & Away fans
in front of the Family Stand
Disabled Toilets: 2 available behind the Family Stand
Contact Nº: (01225) 423087

ADMISSION INFO (1997/98 PRICES)
Adult Standing: £5.00
Adult Seating: £6.50
Child Standing: £3.50
Child Seating: £5.00
Programme Price: £1.20
FAX Number: (01225) 481391

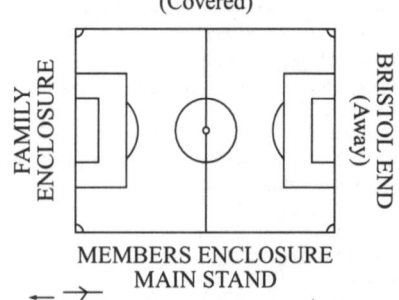

HOME ENCLOSURE
(Covered)

FAMILY ENCLOSURE

BRISTOL END
(Away)

MEMBERS ENCLOSURE
MAIN STAND

Travelling Supporters Information:
Routes: Take the A36 into Bath City Centre. Follow along Pulteney Road then right into Claverton Street and along Lower Bristol Road (A36). Left under railway (1.5 miles) into Twerton High Street and ground on left.

BROMSGROVE ROVERS FC

Founded: 1885
Former Name(s): None
Nickname: 'The Rovers'
Ground: Victoria Ground, Birmingham Road, Bromsgrove, Worcs
Record Attendance: 7,563 (1957/58)

Colours: Shirts - Green & White Stripes
Shorts - Black
Telephone No.: (01527) 876949
Daytime Phone No.: (01527) 876949
Pitch Size: 110 × 72yds
Ground Capacity: 4,893
Seating Capacity: 394

GENERAL INFORMATION
Supporters Club Administrator: Chris Fox
Address: c/o Club
Telephone Number: (01527) 876949
Car Parking: At Ground (200 cars)
Coach Parking: By Police Direction
Nearest Railway Station: Bromsgrove (1.5 miles)
Nearest Bus Station: 500 yards
Club Shop: Yes
Opening Times: Weekdays 9.00am – 1.00pm and also all home matches
Telephone No.: (01527) 876949
Postal Sales: Yes
Nearest Police Station: Bromsgrove Central
Police Force: West Mercia
Police Telephone No.: (01527) 579888

GROUND INFORMATION
Away Supporters' Entrances: –
Away Supporters' Sections: Segregation not usual

DISABLED INFORMATION
Wheelchairs: 6 spaces available (more if necessary) outside the Police Control Room
Disabled Toilets: None
Contact N°: (01527) 876949

ADMISSION INFO (1997/98 PRICES)
Adult Standing: £5.00
Adult Seating: £6.00
Child Standing: £3.00
Child Seating: £4.00
OAP Standing: £3.00
OAP Seating: £4.00
Programme Price: £1.20
FAX Number: (01527) 876949
Note: Young Rovers Members enter free of charge

SEATED STAND

TOWN END TERRACE

NORTH STAND

A38 BIRMINGHAM – WORCESTER ROAD

Travelling Supporters Information:
Routes: From the North: Exit the M42 at junction 1 and follow the A38 towards Bromsgrove. Once in Bromsgrove, at the traffic lights follow Town Centre signs. Victoria Ground is approximately 2 minutes away next to Clark's Motor Services on the right hand side; From the South: Exit the M5 at junction 4 onto the A38. Then as above.

BURTON ALBION FC

Founded: 1950
Former Name(s): None
Nickname: 'The Brewers'
Ground: Eton Park, Princess Way, Burton-on-Trent   DE14 2RU
Record Attendance: 5,860 vs Weymouth FC (1964)

Colours: Shirts - Yellow & Black Stripes
Shorts - Black
Telephone No.: (01283) 565938
Contact No.: (01283) 536510 (Secretary)
Daytime Phone No.: (01283) 565938
Pitch Size: 110 × 72yds
Ground Capacity: 5,000
Seating Capacity: 296

GENERAL INFORMATION
Supporters Club Administrator: Pete Thomas
Address: 67 Hunter Street, Burton-on-Trent, Staffs   DE14 2SR
Telephone Number: (01283) 511983
Car Parking: At Ground (300 cars)
Coach Parking: At Ground
Nearest Railway Station: Burton-on-Trent (1 mile)
Nearest Bus Station: Burton-on-Trent (1 ml)
Club Shop: Yes
Opening Times: Matchdays Only
Telephone No.: (01283) 565938
Postal Sales: Ground
Nearest Police Station: Burton (1 mile)
Police Force: Staffordshire
Police Telephone No.: (01283) 565011

GROUND INFORMATION
Away Supporters' Entrances: Derby Road
Away Supporters' Sections: Gordon Bray Terrace

DISABLED INFORMATION
Wheelchairs: 5 spaces each for home and away fans at the far side of the Main Stand
Disabled Toilets: One available
Contact Nº: (01283) 565938

ADMISSION INFO (1997/98 PRICES)
Adult Standing: £4.00
Adult Seating: £6.00
Child Standing: £2.00
Child Seating: £2.50
Programme Price: £1.00
FAX Number: None

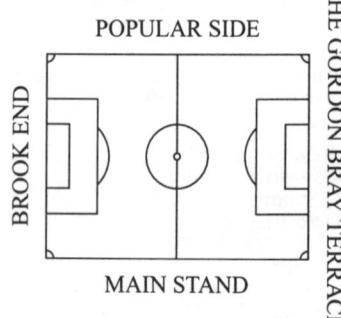

Travelling Supporters Information:
Routes: From the North: Exit the M1 at junction 28 and follow the A38 towards Burton. Take the turning onto A5121 and follow into Burton. Turn right at the island and the ground is on the left; From South: Exit the M1 at junction 22 and follow the A50 towards Burton. Once in Burton go over Trent Bridge and through 3 sets of traffic lights. Turn right at the mini island and continue to the next island where turn left, entrance to the ground is on the left.

CAMBRIDGE CITY FC

Founded: 1908
Former Name(s): Cambridge Town FC
Nickname: 'City Devils'
Ground: City Ground, Milton Road,
Cambridge   CB4 1UY
Record Attendance: 12,058 vs Leytonstone
(1950)

Colours: Shirts - Black & White Halves
Shorts - Black
Telephone No.: (01223) 357973
Daytime Phone No.: (01223) 357973
Pitch Size: 110 × 71yds
Ground Capacity: 5,000
Seating Capacity: 495

GENERAL INFORMATION
Supporters Club Administrator:
Terry Dunn
Address: City Ground, Cambridge
Telephone Number: (01223) 357973
Car Parking: At Ground (200 cars)
Coach Parking: At Ground
Nearest Railway Station: Cambridge (2 mls)
Nearest Bus Station: Cambridge
Club Shop: Yes
Opening Times: Matchdays Only
Telephone No.: (01223) 357973
Postal Sales: Yes
Nearest Police Station: Park Side,
Cambridge
Police Force: Cambridgeshire
Police Telephone No.: (01223) 358966

GROUND INFORMATION
Away Supporters' Entrances: No Segregation
Away Supporters' Sections: No Segregation

DISABLED INFORMATION
Wheelchairs: 6 spaces available in total on Stand Side,
School End
Disabled Toilets: One available in Main Stand
Contact Nº: (01223) 357973

ADMISSION INFO (1997/98 PRICES)
Adult Standing: £5.00
Adult Seating: £5.00
Child Standing: £3.00
Child Seating: £3.00
Programme Price: £1.00
FAX Number: (01223) 460406

```
            ALLOTMENT SIDE
          COVERED STANDING

   W  ┌─────────────────────┐  S
   E  │   ┌───┐     ┌───┐   │  C
   S  │   │   │  ◯  │   │   │  H
   T  │   └───┘     └───┘   │  O
   B  │                     │  O
   R  │                     │  L
   O  │                     │
   O  │                     │  E
   K  └─────────────────────┘  N
   E                            D
   N
   D         MAIN STAND
            CLUBHOUSE
```

Travelling Supporters Information:
Routes: Exit M11 junction 13 and take A1303 into the city. At the end of Madingley Road, turn left into
Chesterton Lane and then Chesterton Road. Go into the one-way system and turn left onto Milton Road (A10)
– ground is on the left.

CRAWLEY TOWN FC

Founded: 1896	**Colours**: Shirts - Red
Former Name(s): None	Shorts - Red
Nickname: 'The Reds'	**Telephone No.**: (01293) 410000 (Ground)
Ground: Broadfield Stadium, Brighton Road,	**Daytime Phone No.**: (01293) 410001 (Office)
Crawley, RH11 9RX	**Contact No.**: (01293) 522371 (Secretary)
Pitch Size: 110 × 72yds	**Ground Capacity**: 4,966
Record Attendance: 2,800 vs Brighton (1997)	**Seating Capacity**: 1,150

GENERAL INFORMATION
Supporters Club Administrator:
Allan Harper
Address: 33 Nuthurst Close, Ifield, Crawley, Sussex
Telephone Number: (01293) 511764
Car Parking: Car Park at Ground (350 cars)
Coach Parking: At Ground
Nearest Railway Station: Crawley (1 mile)
Nearest Bus Station: By Railway Station
Club Shop: At Ground
Opening Times: Daily
Telephone No.: –
Postal Sales: Yes
Nearest Police Station: Kilnmead, Northgate, Crawley (0.75 mile)
Police Force: Sussex
Police Telephone No.: (01293) 524242

GROUND INFORMATION
Away Supporters' Entrances: No segregation normally
Away Supporters' Sections: No segregation
DISABLED INFORMATION
Wheelchairs:
Accommodated in the Disabled Stand (Lift access)
Disabled Toilets: Yes
Contact Nº: (01293) 410001

ADMISSION INFO (1997/98 PRICES)
Adult Standing: £5.00
Adult Seating: £6.00
Child Standing: £3.00
Child Seating: £4.00
Programme Price: £1.00
FAX Number: (01293) 410002

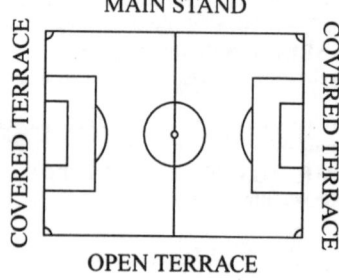

MAIN STAND

COVERED TERRACE

COVERED TERRACE

OPEN TERRACE

Travelling Supporters Information:
Routes: Exit M23 at Junction 11 and take A23 towards Crawley. For 0.25 mile, Stadium on left.

DORCHESTER TOWN FC

Founded: 1880 **Former Name(s)**: None **Nickname**: 'The Magpies' **Ground**: The Avenue Stadium, Weymouth Avenue, Dorchester, Dorset DT1 2RY **Record Attendance**: 4,040 v Chelsea (15/10/90)	**Colours**: Shirts - Black & White Stripes Shorts - Black **Telephone No.**: (01305) 262451/267623 **Daytime Phone No.**: (01305) 264843 **Pitch Size**: 110 × 80yds **Ground Capacity**: 7,210 **Seating Capacity**: 710

GENERAL INFORMATION
Supporters Club Administrator:
H.G. Gill
Address: 39 Thatcham Pk., Yeovil, Somerset
Telephone Number: (01935) 26029
Car Parking: Car Park at Ground (350 cars)
Coach Parking: At Ground
Nearest Railway Station: Dorchester South
& West (both 1 mile)
Nearest Bus Station: Nearby
Club Shop: Yes
Opening Times: During all 1st Team Games
Telephone No.: (01305) 262451
Postal Sales: Yes
Nearest Police Station: Weymouth Avenue,
Dorchester
Police Force: Dorset
Police Telephone No.: (01305) 251212

GROUND INFORMATION
Away Supporters' Entrances: Main Stand Side
Away Supporters' Sections: Not Usually Segregated

DISABLED INFORMATION
Wheelchairs: 10 spaces each for home & away fans at
the North West End of the Terracing
Disabled Toilets: 2 available near the disabled area
Contact Nº: (01305) 262451

ADMISSION INFO (1997/98 PRICES)
Adult Standing: £5.00
Adult Seating: £5.50
Child Standing: £3.00
Child Seating: £3.50
Programme Price: £1.00
FAX Number: (01305) 251569

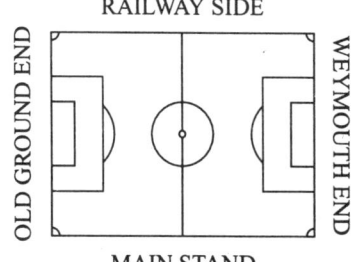

RAILWAY SIDE

OLD GROUND END

WEYMOUTH END

MAIN STAND

Travelling Supporters Information:
Routes: Take Dorchester Bypass (A35) from all directions, ground is on South side of Town adjacent to roundabout at intersection with A354 to Weymouth. Alternatively take Weymouth signs from Town Centre (1.5 miles).

FOREST GREEN ROVERS FC

Founded: 1890
Former Name(s): Stroud FC
Nickname: 'The Rovers'
Ground: The Lawn, Nympsfield Road, Forest Green, Nailsworth, Glos. GL6 0ET
Record Attendance: 2,200 vs Wolves

Colours: Shirts - Black & White Stripes
Shorts - Black
Telephone No.: (01453) 834860
Contact No.: (01453) 834860
Pitch Size: 110 × 70yds
Ground Capacity: 3,132
Seating Capacity: 330

GENERAL INFORMATION
Supporters Club Administrator: Sue Lord
Address: 3 Woodpecker Walk, Forest Green, Nailsworth, GL6 0EJ
Telephone Number: (01453) 835495
Car Parking: At Ground
Coach Parking: At Ground
Nearest Railway Station: Stroud
Nearest Bus Station: Nailsworth
Club Shop: Yes
Opening Times: Matchdays Only
Telephone No.: –
Postal Sales: –
Nearest Police Station: Stroud
Police Force: Gloucestershire
Police Telephone No.: (01452) 521201

GROUND INFORMATION
Away Supporters' Entrances: No normal segregation
Away Supporters' Sections: No segregation normally

DISABLED INFORMATION
Wheelchairs: Accommodated
Disabled Toilets: Yes
Contact Nº: (01453) 834860

ADMISSION INFO (1997/98 PRICES)
Adult Standing: £4.00
Adult Seating: £5.00
Concessionary Standing: £3.00
Concessionary Seating: £4.00
Children under 15: £1.00 (if accompanied)
Children under 15: £2.00 in stand (if accompanied)
Programme Price: £1.00
FAX Number: (01453) 791305

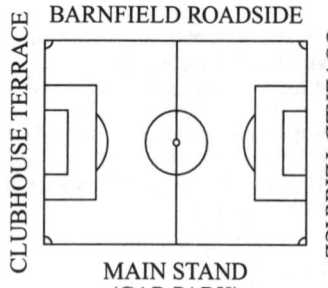

Travelling Supporters Information:
Routes: The Ground is located 4 miles south of Stroud on the A46 to Bath. Upon entering Nailsworth turn into Spring Hill at mini roundabout and Ground is approximately 0.5 mile up the hill on the left.

GLOUCESTER CITY FC

Founded: 1883
Former Name(s): Gloucester YMCA
Nickname: 'The Tigers'
Ground: Meadow Park, Sudmeadow Road, Hempstead, Gloucester   GL2 5HS
Record Attendance: 5,000 (1990)

Colours: Shirts - Yellow & Black Stripes
Shorts - Black
Telephone No.: (01452) 421400
Daytime Phone No.: (01452) 421400
Pitch Size: 112 × 72yds
Ground Capacity: 5,000
Seating Capacity: 560

GENERAL INFORMATION
Supporters Club Administrator: J. Mills
Address: c/o Club
Telephone Number: (01452) 421400
Car Parking: Car Park at Ground (150 cars)
Coach Parking: At Ground
Nearest Railway Station: Gloucester (2 mls)
Nearest Bus Station: Gloucester
Club Shop: Yes
Opening Times: Matchdays Only
Telephone No.: (01452) 421400
Postal Sales: Yes
Nearest Police Station: Gloucester
Police Force: Gloucestershire Constabulary
Police Telephone No.: (01452) 521201

GROUND INFORMATION
Away Supporters' Entrances: Segregation is an option but is normally not used
Away Supporters' Sections: –

DISABLED INFORMATION
Wheelchairs: 6 spaces each for home & away fans alongside the Main Stand
Disabled Toilets: 2 in main toilet block + 1 on other side of the ground
Contact Nº: (01452) 421400

ADMISSION INFO (1997/98 PRICES)
Adult Standing: £5.00
Adult Seating: £6.00
Child Standing: £2.50
Child Seating: £3.50
Programme Price: £1.00
FAX Number: (01452) 301330

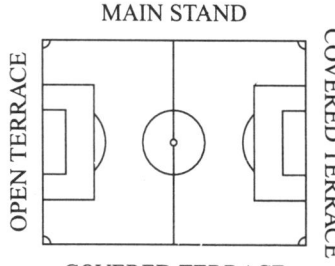

Travelling Supporters Information:
Routes: Take A40 into the City Centre towards Historic Docks, then Severn Road, right into Hempstead Lane then second right into Sudmeadow Road. Ground 50 yards on left.

GRESLEY ROVERS FC

Founded: 1882	**Correspondence Address**: c/o Neil Betteridge,
Former Name(s): None	34 Thorpe Downs Rd, Church
Nickname: 'The Moatmen'	Gresley, Swadlincote, Derbyshire
Ground: The Moat Ground, Moat Street,	**Telephone No.**: (01283) 216315
Church Gresley, Swadlincote, Derbyshire	**Daytime Phone No.**: (01283) 216315
Record Attendance: 3,950 (1957-58)	**Pitch Size**: 110 × 70yds
Colours: Shirts - Red and White Quarters	**Ground Capacity**: 2,000
Shorts - Red	**Seating Capacity**: 415

GENERAL INFORMATION
Supporters Club Administrator: –
Address: c/o Club
Telephone Number: (01283) 216315
Car Parking: At Ground
Coach Parking: At Ground
Nearest Railway Station: Burton-on-Trent (5 miles)
Nearest Bus Station: Swadlincote (1 mile)
Club Shop: Yes
Opening Times: Matchdays Only
Telephone No.: (01283) 216315
Postal Sales: Yes
Nearest Police Station: Swadlincote
Police Force: Derbyshire
Police Telephone No.: (01283) 550101

GROUND INFORMATION
Away Supporters' Entrances: Moat Street or Church Street
Away Supporters' Sections: Not applicable

DISABLED INFORMATION
Wheelchairs: No specific area, but accommodated
Disabled Toilets: None
Contact Nº: (01283) 216315

ADMISSION INFO (1997/98 PRICES)
Adult Standing: £5.00
Adult Seating: £5.00
Child Standing: £2.50
Child Seating: £2.50
Programme Price: £1.00
FAX Number: (01283) 221881

```
                    BASS STAND
  COVERED STANDING                    COVERED STANDING

              COVERED STANDING
                AND SEATING
```

Travelling Supporters Information:
Routes: Take the M42 to A444 Burton-on-Trent exit and head for Castle Gresley. In Castle Gresley at large island, turn right onto the A514 (signposted Church Gresley). Turn right at the top of the hill (Miners Arms) then first left into Church Street. Take 2nd exit on the left (School Street) and Moat Street is next left.

HALESOWEN TOWN FC

Founded: 1873
Former Name(s): None
Nickname: 'The Yeltz'
Ground: The Grove, Old Hawne Lane, Halesowen, West Midlands
Record Attendance: 5,000 (19/11/55)

Colours: Shirts - Black with Yellow Sleeves
Shorts - Black with Yellow Trim
Telephone No.: (0121) 550-2179
Daytime Phone No.: (0121) 550-2179
Pitch Size: 110 × 71yds
Ground Capacity: 5,000
Seating Capacity: 420

GENERAL INFORMATION
Supporters Club Administrator: Paul Floud
Address: 112 Blackberry Lane, Halesowen
Telephone Number: (0121) 550-8999
Car Parking: Room for 70 Cars at Social Club
Coach Parking: Available near Ground
Nearest Railway Station: Old Hill (2 miles) Birmingham New Street (7 miles)
Nearest Bus Station: On main Stourbridge Road.
Club Shop: Yes
Opening Times: Matchdays Only
Telephone No.: (0121) 550-2179
Postal Sales: Yes
Nearest Police Station: Halesowen
Police Force: West Midlands
Police Telephone No.: (0121) 626-8030

GROUND INFORMATION
Away Supporters' Entrances: No segregation
Away Supporters' Sections: No segregation

DISABLED INFORMATION
Wheelchairs: 20 spaces available in total accommodated to each side of the Main Seating Stand
Disabled Toilets: Available near Main Seating Stand
Contact Nº: (0121) 550-2179

ADMISSION INFO (1997/98 PRICES)
Adult Standing: £5.00
Adult Seating: £6.00
Child/OAP Standing: £3.00
Child/OAP Seating: £4.00
Programme Price: £1.00
FAX Number: (0121) 602-0123

```
                 HARRY RUDGE STAND
                      (Seating)
  STOURBRIDGE ROAD END                OLD HAWNE LANE END
      TERRACING                       COVERED TERRACING

                     TERRACING
```

Travelling Supporters Information:
Routes: Exit M5 at junction 3, follow A456 towards Kidderminster to 1st Island and turn right at the signpost onto the A458 towards Dudley. Turn left at the next island and follow the signpost onto A458 towards Stourbridge. At the next island take the 3rd exit, the ground is approximately 400 yards on the left.

HASTINGS TOWN FC

Founded: 1894
Former Name(s): Hastings & St. Leonards
Amateurs
Nickname: 'The Town'
Ground: The Pilot Field, Elphinstone Road,
Hastings   TN34 2AX
Record Attendance: 4,888 (1996/97)

Colours: Shirts - White with Red Trim
     Shorts - White with Red Trim
Telephone No.: (01424) 444635/430517
Daytime Phone No.: (01424) 444635
Contact No.: (01424) 427867 (Secretary)
Pitch Size: 110 × 78yds
Ground Capacity: 10,000
Seating Capacity: 900

GENERAL INFORMATION
Supporters Club Administrator:
R.A. Cosens
Address: 22 Baldslow Road, Hastings
TN34 2EZ
Telephone Number: (01424) 427867
Car Parking: Car Park
Coach Parking: On Street
Nearest Railway Station: Hastings (1.5 mls)
Nearest Bus Station: Town Centre (1.5 miles)
Club Shop: Yes
Opening Times: Match Days Only
Telephone No.: (01424) 852883
Postal Sales: P. Humpreys, c/o Pilot Field
Nearest Police Station: Hastings
Police Force: East Sussex
Police Telephone No.: (01424) 425000

GROUND INFORMATION
Away Supporters' Entrances: No segregation
Away Supporters' Sections: No segregation
DISABLED INFORMATION
Wheelchairs: Arrangements can be made if notified in
advance
Disabled Toilets: None
Contact Nº: (01424) 444635

ADMISSION INFO (1997/98 PRICES)
Adult Standing: £5.00
Adult Seating: £6.00
Child Standing: £3.00
Child Seating: £3.50
Programme Price: £1.00
FAX Number: None

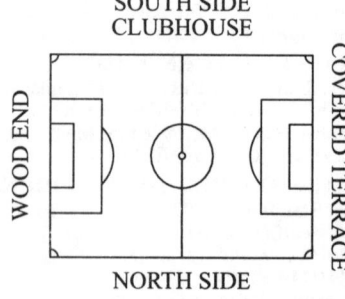

Travelling Supporters Information:
Routes: From A21 turn left into St. Helens Road (A2101). After 1 mile turn left into St. Helens Park Road
which leads into Downs Road. Follow Downs Road to the end then turn left at the T-junction. Ground is on
the right.

KING'S LYNN FC

Founded: 1879	**Colours**: Shirts - Red
Former Name(s): Lynn Town FC	Shorts - Red
Nickname: 'The Linnets'	**Telephone No.**: (01553) 760060
Ground: The Walks Stadium, Tennyson Road,	**Contact No.**: (01945) 583567
King's Lynn PE30 5PB	**Pitch Size**: 115 × 78yds
Record Attendance: 12,937 v Exeter (1950/1)	**Ground Capacity**: 7,500
	Seating Capacity: 1,200

GENERAL INFORMATION
Supporters Club Administrator: None
Address: –
Telephone Number: –
Car Parking: At ground and street parking
Coach Parking: At Ground
Nearest Railway Station: King's Lynn (0.25 mile)
Nearest Bus Station: King's Lynn (0.25 mile)
Club Shop: Yes
Opening Times: Matchdays Only
Telephone No.: (01553) 760060
Postal Sales: Yes
Nearest Police Station: King's Lynn
Police Force: Norfolk
Police Telephone No.: –

GROUND INFORMATION
Away Supporters' Entrances: No segregation
Away Supporters' Sections: No segregation

DISABLED INFORMATION
Wheelchairs: Accommodated
Disabled Toilets: Yes
Contact Nº: (01733) 267272

ADMISSION INFO (1997/98 PRICES)
Adult Standing: £5.00
Adult Seating: £5.00
Child Standing: £2.00 – £3.00
Child Seating: £2.00 – £3.00
Programme Price: £1.20
FAX Number: (01553) 760060

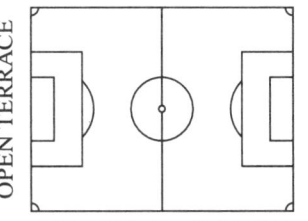

Travelling Supporters Information:
Routes: Take the A17/A47 to King's Lynn roundabout. Follow the road (A47) across the river then take the 1st turning left (signposted South Lynn and Saddlebow) and bear left at flyover into South Lynn and follow road to mini roundabout by Texaco garage. Go straight across keeping Texaco garage on left and continue for 0.5 mile into Tennyson Road and the ground is on the left. If taking the A10 pass Hardwick Industrial Estate and Cemetary follow signposts to town centre and turn right at mini roundabout. Then as above.

MERTHYR TYDFIL FC

Founded: 1945	**Colours**: Shirts - White
Former Name(s): Merthyr Town FC	Shorts - Black
Nickname: 'Martyrs'	**Telephone No.**: (01685) 384102
Ground: Penydarren Park, Merthyr Tydfil,	**Daytime Phone No.**: (01685) 384102
Mid Glamorgan	**Pitch Size**: 110 × 72yds
Record Attendance: 21,000 vs Reading,	**Ground Capacity**: 10,000
F.A. Cup First Round 1949	**Seating Capacity**: 1,500

GENERAL INFORMATION
Supporters Club Administrator: Dave Webb
Address: c/o Club
Telephone Number: (01685) 384102
Car Parking: Street Parking
Coach Parking: Georgetown
Nearest Railway Station: Merthyr Tydfil (0.5 mile)
Nearest Bus Station: Merthyr Tydfil
Club Shop:
Opening Times: Matchdays Only
Telephone No.: (01685) 384102
Postal Sales: Yes
Nearest Police Station: Merthyr Tydfil (0.75 mile)
Police Force: South Wales Constabulary
Police Telephone No.: (01685) 722541

GROUND INFORMATION
Away Supporters' Entrances: Theatre End
Away Supporters' Sections: Theatre End

DISABLED INFORMATION
Wheelchairs: 20 spaces available at the front of the Main Grandstand
Disabled Toilets: Available at Strikers Club
Contact Nº: (01685) 384102

ADMISSION INFO (1997/98 PRICES)
Adult Standing: £5.00
Adult Seating: £5.00
Child Standing: £3.00
Child Seating: £4.00
Programme Price: £1.00
FAX Number: (01685) 382882

COVERED TERRACING (AWAY)

FAMILY STAND

(PANT-MORLAIS ROAD)
THEATRE END

MAIN STAND

Travelling Supporters Information:
Routes: From East: Take A470 into Merthyr. At top of Merthyr High Street, take sharp left at the lights and then 1st right into Brecon Road. Take the 1st right and then 1st right once again and follow the road into the ground; From North: Leave A465 Heads of the Valleys road for Dowlais. After approximately 2 miles, fork right into Brecon Road, take 1st right and then 1st right once again and follow the road into the ground.

NUNEATON BOROUGH FC

Founded: 1937 (Re-formed 1991)	**Colours**: Shirts - Blue & White Stripes
Former Name(s): Nuneaton Town FC	Shorts - White
Nickname: 'The Borough'	**Telephone No.**: (01203) 385738
Ground: Manor Park, Beaumont Road,	**Daytime Phone No.**: (01203) 385738
Nuneaton, Warks CV11 5HD	**Pitch Size**: 110 × 72yds
Record Attendance: 22,114 vs Rotherham	**Ground Capacity**: 6,000
(1967)	**Seating Capacity**: 600

GENERAL INFORMATION
Supporters Club Administrator: −
Address: c/o Club
Telephone Number: −
Car Parking: Street Parking
Coach Parking: At Ground
Nearest Railway Station: Nuneaton (1 mile)
Nearest Bus Station: Nuneaton (1 mile)
Club Shop: Yes − The Boro Shop
Opening Times: Matchdays and also by prior appointment
Telephone No.: (01203) 385738
Postal Sales: Yes
Nearest Police Station: Nuneaton
Police Force: Warwickshire
Police Telephone No.: (01203) 641111

GROUND INFORMATION
Away Supporters' Entrances: Top Cock & Bear Bridge
Away Supporters' Sections: Canal Side

DISABLED SUPPORTERS INFORMATION
Wheelchairs: Accommodated
Disabled Toilets: At rear of Main Stand
Contact Nº: (01203) 385738

ADMISSION INFO (1997/98 PRICES)
Adult Standing: £5.00
Adult Seating: £6.00
Child Standing: £2.50
Child Seating: £3.00
Programme Price: £1.00
FAX Number: (01203) 342690

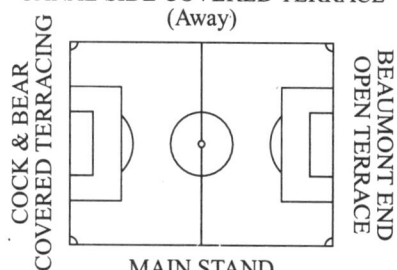

Travelling Supporters Information:
Routes: Exit M6 junction 3 and take A444 to Nuneaton. At roundabout by hospital immediately after pedestrian overbridge turn left into College Street to the Bull Ring. Turn right into Greenmoor Road and follow to end (approximately 0.75 mile) turn right and cross over bridge and ground is on left.

ROTHWELL TOWN FC

Founded: 1896
Former Name(s): Rothwell Town Swifts
Nickname: 'The Bones'
Ground: Cecil Street, Rothwell, Northants, NN14 2EZ
Record Attendance: 2,100 vs Irthlingborough (1971)
Telephone No.: (01536) 710694

Colours: Shirts - Blue & White
          Shorts - Blue & White
Contact Address: R.L. Barratt, 18 Norton Street, Rothwell NN14 6OL
Contact Phone No.: (01536) 507744
Pitch Size: 110 × 72yds
Ground Capacity: 2,000
Seating Capacity: 250

GENERAL INFORMATION
Supporters Club Administrator: None
Address: –
Telephone Number: –
Car Parking: At Ground
Coach Parking: At Ground
Nearest Railway Station: Kettering (4 miles)
Nearest Bus Station: Kettering
Club Shop: Yes
Opening Times: Matchdays Only
Telephone No.: –
Postal Sales: Yes
Nearest Police Station: Kettering
Police Force: Northants.
Police Telephone No.: (01536) 411411

GROUND INFORMATION
Away Supporters' Entrances: No usual segregation
Away Supporters' Sections: No usual segregation

DISABLED INFORMATION
Wheelchairs: No specific area but accommodated
Disabled Toilets: None
Contact Nº: (01536) 710694

ADMISSION INFO (1997/98 PRICES)
Adult Standing: £4.50
Adult Seating: £5.50
Child Standing: £3.00
Child Seating: £3.50
Programme Price: £1.00
FAX Number: (01536) 790227

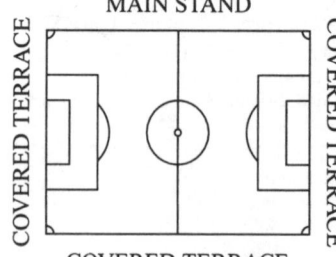

Travelling Supporters Information:
Routes: Take the A14 to Rothwell and turn into Bridge Street at mini roundabout. Take 3rd left into Tresham Street and Ground is at the end on the left.

SALISBURY CITY FC

Founded: 1947	**Colours**: Shirts - White
Former Name(s): Salisbury FC	Shorts - Black
Nickname: 'The Whites'	**Telephone No.**: (01722) 336689
Ground: The Raymond McEnhill Stadium,	**Contact Phone No.**: (01722) 326454
Partridge Way, Old Sarum,	**Pitch Size**: 116 × 74yds
Salisbury, Wiltshire SP1 3ER	**Ground Capacity**: 4,500
Record Attendance: Not known	**Seating Capacity**: 450

GENERAL INFORMATION
Supporters Club Administrator: None
Address: –
Telephone Number: –
Car Parking: At Ground
Coach Parking: At Ground
Nearest Railway Station: Salisbury (2 miles)
Nearest Bus Station: Salisbury
Club Shop: Yes
Opening Times: Office Hours & Matchdays
Telephone No.: –
Postal Sales: Yes
Nearest Police Station: Wilton Road, Salisbury
Police Force: Wiltshire
Police Telephone No.: (01722) 411444

GROUND INFORMATION
Away Supporters' Entrances: Portway End
Away Supporters' Sections: Portway End

DISABLED INFORMATION
Wheelchairs: Accommodated in special section
Disabled Toilets: Yes
Contact Nº: (01722) 326454

ADMISSION INFO (1997/98 PRICES)
Adult Standing: £4.00
Adult Seating: £5.00
Child Standing: £2.50
Child Seating: £3.50
Programme Price: £1.20
FAX Number: (01980) 626855

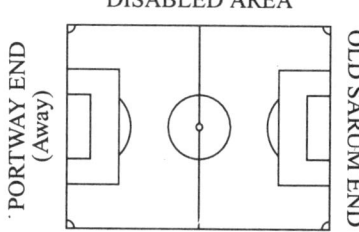

MAIN STAND
DISABLED AREA

PORTWAY END
(Away)

OLD SARUM END

Travelling Supporters Information:
Routes: The stadium is situated off the main A345 Salisbury to Amesbury Road on the northern edge of the city, 2 miles from the City Centre.

SITTINGBOURNE FC

Founded: 1881
Former Name(s): Sittingbourne United FC
Nickname: 'The Brickies', 'The Bourne'
Ground: Central Park, Eurolink, Sittingbourne, Kent   ME10 3SB
Record Attendance: 6,000 vs Tottenham Hotspur (1993)

Colours: Shirts - Red
        Shorts - Black
Telephone No.: (01795) 435077
Daytime Phone No.: (01795) 435077
Pitch Size: 120 × 82yds
Ground Capacity: 7,600
Seating Capacity: 2,000

GENERAL INFORMATION
Supporters Club Administrator: Ann Morrison
Address: c/o Club
Telephone Number: –
Car Parking: At Ground
Coach Parking: At Ground
Nearest Railway Station: Sittingbourne (0.75 mile)
Nearest Bus Station: Sittingbourne
Club Shop: Yes
Opening Times: Daily
Telephone No.: (01795) 435077
Postal Sales: Yes
Nearest Police Station: Sittingbourne
Police Force: Kent Constabulary
Police Telephone No.: (01795) 477055

GROUND INFORMATION
Away Supporters' Entrances: No segregation
Away Supporters' Sections: No segregation

DISABLED INFORMATION
Wheelchairs: Accommodated
Disabled Toilets: –
Contact Nº: (01795) 435077

ADMISSION INFO (1997/98 PRICES)
Adult Standing: £5.00
Adult Seating: £6.00
Child Standing: £3.00
Child Seating: £4.00
Programme Price: £1.00
FAX Number: None

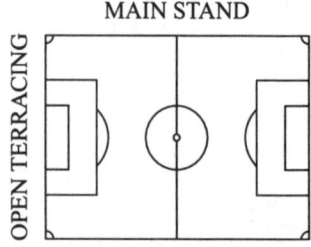

Travelling Supporters Information:
Routes: Take A2 into Sittingbourne Town Centre and follow one-way system into St. Michaels Road, then follow signs for ground.

ST. LEONARDS STAMCROFT FC

Founded: 1971
Former Name(s): Stamco RC
Nickname: 'The Blues'
Ground: The Firs, Elphinstone Road,
Hastings, E. Sussex   TN34 2AX
Record Attendance: 1,798 vs Tiverton Town
(15/1/95)

Colours: Shirts - Blue
Shorts - White
Contact No.: (01424) 434755
Pitch Size: 112 × 72yds
Ground Capacity: 3,816
Seating Capacity: 251

Photo: Picture Express St. Leonards

GENERAL INFORMATION
Supporters Club Administrator: None
Address: –
Telephone Number: –
Car Parking: At Ground (180 cars)
Coach Parking: At Ground
Nearest Railway Station: Hastings (2 miles)
Nearest Bus Station: Hastings (2 miles)
Club Shop: Yes
Opening Times: Office Hours & Matchdays
Telephone No.: –
Postal Sales: Yes
Nearest Police Station: Hastings
Police Force: East Sussex
Police Telephone No.: (01424) 425000

GROUND INFORMATION
Away Supporters' Entrances: No segregation
Away Supporters' Sections: No segregation

DISABLED INFORMATION
Wheelchairs: Accommodated
Disabled Toilets: Yes
The Blind: No Special Facilities

ADMISSION INFO (1997/98 PRICES)
Adult Standing: £4.00
Adult Seating: £4.50
Child Standing: £2.00
Child Seating: £2.50
Concessionary Standing: £2.00
Concessionary Seating: £2.50
FAX Number: (01424) 716362/440505
Programme Price: £1.00

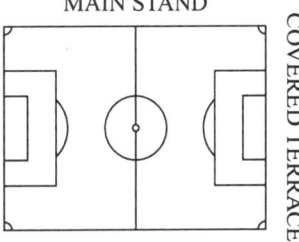

Travelling Supporters Information:
Routes: Take the A21 to Hastings and opposite 'Do-It-All' turn right into Junction Road. At T-Junction turn right into The Ridge. Go straight across 2 roundabouts and, after 2 miles, turn right into Elphinstone Road opposite Cemetary.

SUDBURY TOWN FC

Founded: 1885
Former Name(s): None
Nickname: 'The Borough'
Ground: Priory Stadium, Priory Walk, Sudbury
Suffolk   CO10 6AP
Record Attendance: 4,700 vs Ipswich Town
(Testimonial) (1978)

Colours: Shirts - Yellow
Shorts - Yellow
Telephone No.: (01787) 370957 (Manager)
Contact No.: (01787) 372352 (Secretary)
Pitch Size: 110 × 80yds
Ground Capacity: 5,000
Seating Capacity: 263

GENERAL INFORMATION
Supporters Club Administrator:
Paul Haighton
Address: c/o Club
Telephone Number: (01787) 370957
Car Parking: At Ground
Coach Parking: At Ground
Nearest Railway Station: Sudbury (0.75 ml)
Nearest Bus Station: Sudbury (0.5 mile)
Club Shop: Yes
Opening Times: Matchdays Only
Telephone No.: (01787) 370957
Postal Sales: Yes – via Darren Witt, 4 Highfield Road, Sudbury, Suffolk   CO10 6QJ
Nearest Police Station: Sudbury (1 mile)
Police Force: Suffolk
Police Telephone No.: (01284) 774300

GROUND INFORMATION
Away Supporters' Entrances: No segregation
Away Supporters' Sections: No segregation

DISABLED INFORMATION
Wheelchairs: Accommodated around the ground
Disabled Toilets: None
Contact Nº: (01787) 370957

ADMISSION INFO (1997/98 PRICES)
Adult Standing: £5.00
Adult Seating: £4.00
Child Standing: £3.00
Child Seating: £2.00
Programme Price: £1.00
FAX Number: (01787) 370957

```
        CLUBHOUSE
ORCHARD    WHEELERS
  STAND       STAND

R                      Q
I                      U
V                      A
E                      Y
R                      L
                       A
E                      N
N                      E
D                      E
                       N
                       D
        MAIN STAND
```

Travelling Supporters Information:
Routes: From North: Take A134 into town centre then turn into Friar Street. Pass cricket ground and continue to the 'Ship & Star'. Turn left into Priory Walk for ground; From South: Take A131 from Halstead into Sudbury – turn right over river bridge (30 yards) – follow to 'Ship & Star' pub and turn right into Priory Walk.

TAMWORTH FC

Founded: 1933	**Colours**: Shirts - Red
Former Name(s): None	Shorts - Black
Nickname: 'The Lambs' or 'The Town'	**Telephone No.**: (01827) 65798
Ground: The Lamb Ground, Kettlebrook,	**Daytime Phone No.**: (01827) 66786
Tamworth B79 1HA	**Pitch Size**: 110 × 70yds
Record Attendance: 4,920 vs Atherton Town	**Ground Capacity**: 2,500
(3/4/48)	**Seating Capacity**: 400

GENERAL INFORMATION
Supporters Club Administrator: None
Address: –
Telephone Number: –
Car Parking: At Ground (100 cars)
Coach Parking: At Ground
Nearest Railway Station: Tamworth (0.5 mile)
Nearest Bus Station: Tamworth
Club Shop: Yes
Opening Times: Matchdays
Telephone No.: (01827) 65798
Postal Sales: Yes
Nearest Police Station: Tamworth
Police Telephone No.: (01827) 61001

GROUND INFORMATION
Away Supporters' Entrances: Usually no segregation
Away Supporters' Sections: –

DISABLED INFORMATION
Wheelchairs: Accommodated
Disabled Toilets: None
Contact Nº: (01827) 65798

ADMISSION INFO (1997/98 PRICES)
Adult Standing: £5.00
Adult Seating: £6.00
Child Standing: £2.50
Child Seating: £3.50
Programme Price: £1.00
FAX Number: (01827) 66786

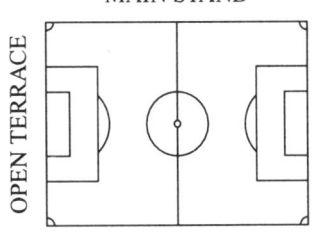

MAIN STAND

OPEN TERRACE

COVERED TERRACE

COVERED TERRACE

Travelling Supporters Information:
Routes: Exit the M42 at Junction 10 and take the A5/A51 to Town Centre following signs Town Centre/ Snowdome. Then follow signs for Kettlebrook and Ground is in Kettlebrook Road, 50 yards from the traffic island by the Railway Viaduct and the 'Snowdome'.

WORCESTER CITY FC

Founded: 1902
Former Name(s): Berwick Rangers
Nickname: 'The City'
Ground: St. Georges Lane, Worcester,
WR1 1QT
Record Attendance: 17,042 vs Sheffield Utd.
(1958/59)

Colours: Shirts - Blue & White Stripes
Shorts - Blue
Telephone No.: (01905) 23003
Daytime Phone No.: (01905) 23003
Pitch Size: 110 × 73yds
Ground Capacity: 4,749
Seating Capacity: 1,223

GENERAL INFORMATION
Supporters Club Administrator:
R.I. Widdowson
Address: 8 Upper Ground, Long Meadow,
Warndon Villages, Worcester
Telephone Number: –
Car Parking: Street Parking
Coach Parking: Street Parking
Nearest Railway Station: Foregate Street/
Shrub Hill
Nearest Bus Station: Crowngate Bus Station
Club Shop: At Ground
Opening Times: Matchdays (45 mins before
kick-off and during game)
Telephone No.: (01905) 23003
Postal Sales: Yes
Nearest Police Station: Deansway
Police Force: West Mercia Constabulary
Police Telephone No.: (01905) 723888

GROUND INFORMATION
Away Supporters' Entrances: When segregated –
turnstile at Canal End
Away Supporters' Sections: Canal End

DISABLED INFORMATION
Wheelchairs: Accommodated by arrangement
Disabled Toilets: None
Contact Nº: (01905) 23003

ADMISSION INFO (1997/98 PRICES)
Adult Standing: £5.00
Adult Seating: £5.50
Child Standing: £3.00
Child Seating: £3.50
Programme Price: £1.00
FAX Number: (01905) 26668

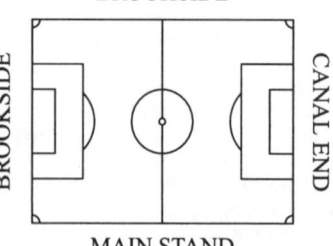

BROOKSIDE

BROOKSIDE

CANAL END

MAIN STAND

Travelling Supporters Information:
Routes: From North & East: Exit M5 junction 5 and follow A38 through Droitwich into Worcester. Take a left turn 500 yards after 1st set of traffic lights (signposted); From South & West: Exit M5 junction 7 and follow A44 into Worcester, go past Racecourse and follow A38 towards Bromsgrove. Right turn signposted.

GM Vauxhall Conference Season 1996/97	Altrincham	Bath City	Bromsgrove Rovers	Dover Athletic	Farnborough Town	Gateshead	Halifax Town	Hayes	Hednesford Town	Kettering Town	Kidderminster Harriers	Macclesfield Town	Morecambe	Northwich Victoria	Rushden & Diamonds	Slough Town	Southport	Stalybridge Celtic	Stevenage Borough	Telford United	Welling United	Woking
Altrincham		1-3	3-1	1-2	0-3	0-1	2-1	0-2	1-1	4-3	0-1	0-1	0-1	2-3	4-3	0-1	1-0	1-0	1-2	2-3	1-1	1-1
Bath City	1-2		1-0	2-1	1-1	3-0	0-0	3-1	2-1	0-2	0-3	0-3	2-1	3-2	3-2	0-0	0-2	0-2	0-0	2-3	3-1	1-1
Bromsgrove Rvrs.	4-0	2-1		3-1	1-1	2-2	3-0	2-2	1-0	1-2	0-1	0-3	2-3	0-5	0-1	4-1	0-1	0-1	1-1	2-1	1-0	0-3
Dover Athletic	2-2	2-2	2-0		0-0	0-1	2-2	1-0	2-2	0-1	0-5	2-1	3-0	2-2	1-1	0-0	0-1	2-1	3-3	1-4	2-1	5-1
Farnborough Tn.	1-1	4-1	2-1	2-3		1-2	3-0	1-1	1-0	0-2	2-1	0-1	2-2	2-2	2-2	2-1	3-3	1-0	3-1	0-2	2-1	1-2
Gateshead	1-1	5-0	1-0	1-3	1-0		0-1	1-1	0-1	1-1	3-1	0-0	0-3	5-1	1-0	2-1	2-2	0-2	2-2	2-3	1-2	3-2
Halifax Town	1-1	4-5	1-0	1-3	3-0	2-0		2-2	1-0	2-1	2-3	3-3	1-1	0-3	1-3	4-1	2-0	4-1	4-2	0-3	1-1	0-4
Hayes	3-1	0-1	1-0	2-0	0-0	0-0	0-0		4-0	2-1	0-1	0-2	2-3	1-1	1-1	5-0	1-1	0-2	1-3	0-1	1-1	3-2
Hednesford Town	2-2	2-0	3-0	1-1	0-1	0-0	1-1	2-0		0-0	1-4	4-1	2-1	3-0	1-0	2-1	0-1	2-1	0-0	0-0	0-3	2-0
Kettering Town	3-1	1-0	2-0	1-1	3-1	4-1	4-1	2-2	0-2		3-1	1-4	0-2	1-0	1-5	0-0	0-1	1-0	1-2	0-1	2-3	0-0
Kidderminster H.	1-1	6-0	1-2	4-1	2-3	3-2	3-0	5-1	2-1	4-0		0-0	2-2	1-0	1-0	1-2	3-0	1-1	3-0	1-0	3-2	1-0
Macclesfield Tn.	1-1	2-2	4-0	1-0	3-0	3-0	1-0	1-0	4-0	2-0	0-1		0-0	0-1	2-1	2-0	3-2	2-0	2-1	2-1	1-1	5-0
Morecambe	2-1	1-1	1-0	3-1	3-0	4-0	1-1	2-4	2-2	5-2	2-3	1-0		2-0	2-0	0-0	2-3	0-0	1-2	0-1	1-2	1-2
Northwich Vict.	2-2	1-0	1-0	2-0	1-1	4-2	2-2	2-1	2-1	2-1	1-1	2-1	1-0		1-2	0-1	5-1	0-1	0-1	1-0	0-0	1-2
Rushden & Diam.	3-2	4-1	1-2	1-1	0-2	0-4	1-0	2-2	0-2	1-0	1-1	1-1	2-1	1-1		2-2	3-0	1-1	0-1	2-0	3-0	1-1
Slough Town	0-1	5-2	2-0	2-2	1-1	0-1	1-0	1-3	2-2	1-1	0-2	0-0	1-2	3-4	5-0		1-1	4-1	1-6	6-0	3-3	3-0
Southport	1-3	3-1	0-0	0-1	0-3	1-1	2-1	0-2	1-2	2-2	1-0	1-5	3-1	0-0	2-1	0-1		3-0	0-0	0-1	3-2	4-1
Stalybridge Celtic	1-0	2-2	3-0	4-2	2-0	2-5	2-3	3-1	1-2	3-1	4-1	0-1	2-1	0-1	2-0	2-2	2-2		0-3	0-0	0-0	0-2
Stevenage Boro'	2-1	2-1	3-0	4-1	2-3	4-1	6-0	2-0	3-2	0-0	2-2	2-3	4-2	2-0	4-1	2-2	2-1	1-1		3-0	2-1	0-3
Telford United	0-0	1-1	3-1	1-0	2-0	0-3	1-1	0-0	1-1	1-0	0-2	0-3	2-3	2-2	0-5	0-2	1-0	1-1	2-3		2-0	1-2
Welling United	1-0	2-0	1-2	1-0	0-2	2-0	0-1	1-0	1-2	1-2	0-1	0-3	1-4	1-1	0-1	3-2	0-1	2-0	2-0	2-1		1-1
Woking	7-1	2-2	1-3	1-1	0-2	1-1	2-2	1-2	2-0	2-1	2-1	2-3	1-2	3-1	4-2	2-0	0-1	3-2	3-1	0-0	2-1	

GM VAUXHALL CONFERENCE 1996/97

FINAL LEAGUE TABLE

Macclesfield Town	42	27	9	6	80	30	90
Kidderminster Harriers	42	26	7	9	84	42	85
Stevenage Borough	42	24	10	8	87	53	82
Morecambe	42	19	9	14	69	56	66
Woking	42	18	10	14	71	63	64
Northwich Victoria	42	17	12	13	61	54	63
Farnborough Town	42	16	13	13	58	53	61
Hednesford Town	42	16	12	14	52	50	60
Telford United	42	16	10	16	46	56	58
Gateshead	42	15	11	16	59	63	56
Southport	42	15	10	17	51	61	55
Rushden & Diamonds	42	14	11	17	61	63	53
Stalybridge Celtic	42	14	10	18	53	58	52
Kettering Town	42	14	9	19	53	62	51
Hayes	42	12	14	16	54	55	50
Slough Town	42	12	14	16	62	65	50
Dover Athletic	42	12	14	16	57	68	50
Welling United	42	13	9	20	50	60	48
Halifax Town	42	12	12	18	55	74	48
Bath City	42	12	11	19	53	80	47
Bromsgrove Rovers	42	12	5	25	41	67	41
Altrincham	42	9	12	21	49	73	39

Promoted : – Macclesfield Town
Relegated : – Bath City, Bromsgrove Rovers & Altrincham

ICIS Premier Division Season 1996/97	Aylesbury United	Bishops Stortford	Boreham wood	Bromley	Carshalton Athletic	Chertsey Town	Dagenham & Redbridge	Dulwich Hamlet	Enfield	Grays Athletic	Harrow Borough	Hendon	Heybridge Swifts	Hitchin Town	Kingstonian	Oxford City	Purfleet	St. Albans	Staines Town	Sutton United	Yeading	Yeovil Town
Aylesbury United		2-2	2-0	1-1	3-1	2-1	0-1	2-0	1-3	3-0	2-0	1-2	1-0	2-1	2-5	6-1	0-2	2-1	2-1	3-3	2-2	0-0
Bishops Stortford	2-0		0-0	4-3	2-1	3-1	2-0	0-1	1-3	0-0	0-1	2-1	0-0	1-2	2-2	2-2	2-3	1-1	1-0	2-5	1-1	0-1
Boreham Wood	1-1	4-1		2-2	3-0	1-2	3-1	2-2	1-1	2-1	2-0	1-2	0-0	4-0	0-0	3-2	0-1	0-2	3-0	1-0	1-1	0-3
Bromley	0-2	2-1	2-0		2-0	5-1	1-0	0-0	0-2	1-2	1-2	2-2	1-1	3-2	2-2	3-0	2-1	1-1	1-2	2-1	5-1	1-2
Carshalton Ath.	3-1	1-0	1-2	3-2		2-0	0-0	0-0	0-1	6-0	2-1	0-2	4-1	1-2	1-3	1-1	2-1	2-0	2-0	3-3	0-0	0-1
Chertsey Town	0-0	0-3	1-1	3-1	2-3		0-3	0-2	1-1	0-6	2-2	1-0	3-5	0-5	0-3	2-4	0-1	0-5	3-2	1-1	2-1	0-2
Dag'ham & Red.	0-2	3-0	2-1	0-2	0-1	2-1		1-1	0-2	2-1	3-1	1-1	3-0	1-1	2-0	4-2	2-0	0-1	3-0	2-1	1-2	0-1
Dulwich Hamlet	1-1	2-0	2-1	2-1	4-1	3-0	0-2		0-1	3-0	0-0	2-1	1-3	2-2	1-2	0-1	2-1	1-2	0-2	0-1	0-1	4-1
Enfield	3-0	1-1	3-0	4-3	2-0	5-0	0-1	2-3		4-0	1-0	2-2	1-2	1-0	3-0	3-3	3-0	1-0	4-0	3-1	1-1	3-0
Grays Athletic	2-0	0-1	2-4	1-0	0-1	0-2	0-3	1-1	0-2		3-2	0-0	0-1	2-2	1-1	1-1	0-1	1-2	1-2	1-1	1-2	2-3
Harrow Borough	0-0	1-1	2-0	2-0	1-1	1-0	1-1	2-1	1-1	1-0		2-2	3-3	3-1	1-2	2-3	3-1	0-1	0-2	2-1	0-1	2-3
Hendon	0-3	3-1	1-2	4-1	2-2	1-0	2-1	2-2	0-3	0-1	2-1		1-1	1-0	2-1	2-0	2-3	0-2	1-1	1-2	1-1	1-3
Heybridge Swifts	1-3	0-0	0-2	4-3	0-2	4-1	4-1	1-1	0-0	3-0	0-0	1-1		2-1	2-1	2-1	1-3	2-1	2-1	3-3	0-5	0-0
Hitchin Town	2-1	3-0	1-2	5-2	3-2	2-1	0-0	0-0	0-3	0-2	2-4	1-2	1-2		4-1	4-2	2-0	1-1	2-1	2-5	3-1	0-1
Kingstonian	0-1	0-1	5-1	1-1	1-1	2-0	2-3	4-2	0-1	5-2	4-4	2-1	1-0	3-1		4-1	3-2	0-1	3-3	2-3	4-2	0-3
Oxford City	3-2	4-1	0-0	2-3	1-1	0-2	2-2	1-1	1-4	1-1	2-1	2-0	1-2	5-1	3-1		1-2	3-2	1-0	1-3	0-1	0-2
Purfleet	0-1	3-0	1-1	2-0	2-0	2-0	2-2	1-4	1-3	2-4	2-0	0-0	3-3	1-1	3-2	2-2		2-2	2-0	3-2	2-2	1-1
St. Albans	0-0	1-1	0-2	0-3	0-0	4-5	0-2	2-2	1-4	4-2	2-2	1-0	4-2	2-1	2-0	0-1	2-1		3-0	1-1	0-0	2-3
Staines Town	3-1	0-0	2-1	3-0	2-0	0-0	0-0	1-3	0-2	3-1	1-1	0-3	2-2	1-2	2-1	1-2	1-3	1-2		2-3	2-3	1-1
Sutton United	3-3	2-1	1-1	2-2	2-0	4-2	2-1	2-0	1-1	1-1	3-3	3-1	0-2	4-3	5-2	1-2	0-0	2-3	2-0		3-0	0-3
Yeading	0-1	3-0	2-1	1-0	0-0	0-0	1-1	3-0	1-1	3-0	1-2	2-1	1-0	0-1	5-1	4-1	1-1	0-3	1-0	1-2		0-0
Yeovil Town	3-2	1-0	0-0	1-0	3-0	4-0	0-0	6-1	2-2	2-0	2-1	2-0	1-0	1-0	2-3	4-1	4-3	3-1	3-1	3-2	2-0	

ICIS PREMIER DIVISION 1996/97

FINAL LEAGUE TABLE

Yeovil Town	42	31	8	3	83	34	101
Enfield	42	28	11	3	91	29	95
Sutton United	42	18	13	11	87	70	67
Dagenham & Red.	42	18	11	13	57	43	65
Yeading	42	17	14	11	58	47	65
St. Albans City	42	18	11	13	65	55	65
Aylesbury United	42	18	11	13	64	54	65
Purfleet	42	17	11	14	67	63	62
Heybridge Swifts	42	16	14	12	62	62	62
Boreham Wood	42	15	13	14	56	52	58
Kingstonian	42	16	8	18	79	79	56
Dulwich Hamlet	42	14	13	15	57	57	55
Carshalton Athletic	42	14	11	17	51	56	53
Hitchin Town	42	15	7	20	67	73	52
Oxford City	42	14	10	18	67	83	52
Hendon	42	13	12	17	53	59	51
Harrow Borough	42	12	14	16	58	62	50
Bromley	42	13	9	20	67	72	48
Bishop's Stortford	42	10	13	19	43	64	43
Staines Town	42	10	8	24	46	71	38
Grays Athletic	42	8	9	25	43	78	33
Chertsey Town	42	8	7	27	40	98	31

Promoted : Yeovil Town
Relegated : Staines Town, Grays Athletic & Chertsey Town

Unibond League Premier Division Season 1996/97	Accrington Stanley	Alfreton Town	Bamber Bridge	Barrow	Bishop Auckland	Blyth Spartans	Boston United	Buxton	Chorley	Colwyn Bay	Emley	Frickley Athletic	Gainsborough Trinity	Guiseley	Hyde United	Knowsley United	Lancaster City	Leek Town	Marine	Runcorn	Spennymoor United	Winsford United
Accrington Stan.		4-2	4-1	1-2	1-4	2-3	3-1	5-3	0-3	3-1	1-1	4-0	0-4	1-2	3-2	1-1	2-1	1-2	1-0	2-2	2-0	0-0
Alfreton Town	1-3		2-1	2-3	1-1	1-2	1-2	1-2	0-3	2-1	0-0	1-0	0-1	4-5	0-3	2-0	1-0	1-1	0-1	1-1	2-1	1-1
Bamber Bridge	1-1	2-2		1-3	1-2	0-1	0-2	2-2	0-2	2-3	0-3	5-1	1-1	6-4	1-4	1-2	0-2	0-4	1-0	0-5	1-3	1-2
Barrow	4-3	3-0	1-1		0-1	2-2	0-1	0-0	3-0	1-0	3-0	2-0	2-2	1-1	1-1	1-1	3-0	3-0	0-1	1-1	1-0	2-1
Bishop Auckland	1-1	2-2	2-0	0-1		1-3	1-0	5-0	1-3	3-1	0-1	2-2	3-3	1-0	3-0	4-1	4-2	1-1	2-2	2-0	4-1	2-0
Blyth Spartans	1-1	2-1	2-1	1-0	0-0		1-2	5-0	1-3	0-0	1-1	6-3	1-1	1-1	2-1	6-0	3-1	0-1	1-1	3-2	2-0	1-2
Boston United	3-1	1-1	1-1	3-5	1-1	2-1		3-0	3-0	3-2	4-1	2-3	1-1	1-1	0-0	1-0	4-2	0-2	2-0	2-2	2-0	2-0
Buxton	1-3	0-1	0-1	0-1	1-1	1-2	0-2		0-1	2-2	0-3	1-3	2-1	0-1	0-3	0-0	1-0	0-2	0-2	0-2	0-2	1-2
Chorley	1-1	2-1	1-3	1-3	1-1	1-3	3-4	2-2		4-0	1-2	0-1	3-4	1-0	3-3	2-2	0-2	0-0	2-1	4-0	1-0	0-1
Colwyn Bay	0-2	1-4	5-2	1-2	1-2	3-0	1-5	3-4	1-1		3-2	5-0	0-2	1-1	1-3	5-0	1-1	3-1	0-0	3-3	1-1	1-2
Emley	3-1	4-0	1-2	3-0	2-0	3-2	1-1	3-0	1-0	0-1		3-3	3-3	4-0	2-4	2-4	2-2	2-3	5-1	2-1	3-0	1-1
Frickley Athletic	0-1	7-2	1-0	0-2	0-4	2-2	2-2	3-1	2-1	3-4	1-2		2-2	0-1	0-3	0-2	3-1	2-3	0-1	1-1	5-2	3-2
Gainsborough T.	2-2	3-0	0-2	3-0	0-1	0-1	1-1	1-1	3-0	2-0	0-3	2-0		1-0	0-1	2-0	1-1	0-1	4-1	1-0	2-0	
Guiseley	1-0	1-1	5-0	1-3	0-0	2-1	1-0	2-0	1-4	0-1	2-0	1-0	1-0		2-3	1-0	1-1	2-0	0-1	0-1	2-1	1-1
Hyde United	7-2	5-0	2-2	1-0	1-1	0-2	2-2	2-0	3-2	1-1	1-2	5-1	2-1	2-2		4-0	0-0	3-1	1-1	2-0	4-0	0-0
Knowsley United	1-1	1-1	5-0	0-3	0-5	0-1	0-0	4-1	4-1	3-0	0-1	0-0	0-1	2-2	3-3		3-1	3-2	3-1	1-1	2-2	0-3
Lancaster City	1-2	1-0	2-3	1-0	2-1	1-0	0-1	1-0	4-1	1-1	1-3	1-3	0-2	1-2	0-4	2-2		0-3	0-2	0-2	1-0	1-1
Leek Town	2-1	4-0	4-1	2-1	1-0	4-0	1-0	1-1	1-0	1-0	0-0	3-0	1-0	1-3	0-0	2-0	2-1		0-1	1-1	1-1	3-1
Marine	2-1	1-1	2-0	1-1	2-3	0-3	1-0	3-0	1-0	0-0	0-0	3-1	2-0	1-2	1-1	2-2	5-1	0-0		1-0	1-0	3-0
Runcorn	1-3	1-0	1-2	0-0	1-3	1-0	1-1	1-1	0-2	5-0	1-1	0-0	2-1	2-0	1-3	1-0	3-2	0-2	1-1		1-0	4-3
Spennymoor Utd.	0-0	3-2	2-1	1-2	1-5	0-2	1-3	0-1	0-0	1-2	2-3	3-1	1-2	4-1	1-1	5-0	1-1	0-1	0-0	6-0		2-0
Winsford United	1-1	1-0	4-2	1-2	1-2	0-2	0-1	1-1	0-1	3-0	2-2	1-0	1-1	1-1	2-1	3-1	0-1	0-2	0-1	0-0	1-1	

UNIBOND LEAGUE PREMIER DIVISION
SEASON 1996/97

FINAL LEAGUE TABLE

Team	P	W	D	L	F	A	Pts
Leek Town	44	28	9	7	71	35	93
Bishop Auckland	44	23	14	7	88	43	83
Hyde United	44	22	16	6	93	46	82
Emley	44	23	12	9	89	54	81
Barrow	44	23	11	10	71	45	80
Boston United	44	22	13	9	74	47	79
Blyth Spartans	44	22	11	11	74	49	77
Marine	44	20	15	9	53	37	75
Guiseley	44	20	11	13	63	54	71
Gainsborough Trin.	44	18	12	14	65	46	66
Accrington Stanley	44	18	12	14	77	70	66
Runcorn	44	15	15	14	63	62	60
Chorley	44	16	9	19	69	66	57
Winsford United	44	13	14	17	50	56	53
Knowsley United	44	12	14	18	58	79	49
Colwyn Bay	44	11	13	20	60	76	46
Lancaster City	44	12	9	23	48	75	45
Frickley Athletic	44	12	8	24	62	91	44
Spennymoor United	44	10	10	24	52	68	40
Bamber Bridge	44	11	7	26	59	99	40
Alfreton Town	44	8	13	23	45	83	37
Witton Albion	44	5	14	25	41	91	29
Buxton	44	5	12	27	33	86	27

Promoted : – Leek Town
Relegated : – Witton Albion and Buxton

Dr. Marten's Football League Premier Division Season 1996/97	Ashford Town	Atherstone United	Baldock Town	Burton Albion	Cambridge City	Chelmsford City	Cheltenham Town	Crawley Town	Dorchester Town	Gloucester City	Gravesend & Northfleet	Gresley Rovers	Halesowen Town	Hastings Town	King's Lynn	Merthyr Tydfil	Newport AFC	Nuneaton Borough	Salisbury City	Sittingbourne	Sudbury Town	Worcester City
Ashford Town	■	0-3	2-2	3-3	2-2	1-0	1-1	3-3	2-1	0-3	1-1	1-3	1-1	3-3	4-0	0-1	1-1	2-0	0-1	1-1	2-2	0-0
Atherstone Utd.	1-1	■	1-3	2-1	1-0	1-1	0-0	2-0	2-1	0-0	0-0	0-1	0-5	0-0	1-1	3-4	1-0	0-0	4-0	2-1	1-0	2-2
Baldock Town	1-1	0-2	■	1-3	0-3	4-1	1-0	1-2	2-1	2-3	0-5	0-3	0-1	2-0	1-1	2-2	1-0	1-2	1-1	1-5	3-2	0-3
Burton Albion	1-0	1-2	1-1	■	3-3	4-2	0-0	2-0	4-1	3-1	1-3	2-3	0-0	0-0	4-1	0-1	3-0	2-0	1-1	1-0	2-1	2-2
Cambridge City	4-0	1-2	1-1	1-0	■	1-0	1-4	4-0	2-2	0-1	4-2	1-4	1-3	0-2	2-2	0-0	2-2	1-1	1-3	1-3	1-2	
Chelmsford City	1-1	0-1	2-3	2-2	2-0	■	2-4	1-0	1-1	1-3	4-0	2-2	3-0	2-2	0-2	0-0	1-1	3-1	1-2	1-4	1-3	1-2
Cheltenham Tn.	6-0	2-0	3-2	3-3	1-0	1-0	■	1-2	1-1	1-1	0-1	2-2	2-1	1-0	1-2	2-0	0-0	0-2	0-2	2-0	0-2	2-0
Crawley Town	2-3	2-0	2-0	0-2	0-2	1-2	3-3	■	2-0	1-1	0-2	0-0	0-3	0-2	0-0	1-0	1-3	1-0	2-2	2-2	1-2	2-1
Dorchester Town	0-2	1-0	3-2	5-0	0-2	1-0	1-3	2-5	■	2-2	2-2	1-3	1-1	1-1	3-0	2-0	1-3	4-2	2-0	0-1	2-0	
Gloucester City	6-1	0-0	3-1	2-4	2-0	3-1	2-1	2-1	3-1	■	3-1	1-2	0-3	2-0	1-0	6-3	2-1	1-0	1-3	1-1	3-3	1-1
Gravesend & N.	1-3	1-0	1-2	0-1	1-1	1-0	1-3	2-0	1-3	2-3	■	2-1	1-3	2-0	2-2	0-0	3-0	1-1	3-2	3-0	4-2	2-0
Gresley Rovers	2-2	1-1	3-0	1-1	3-1	2-2	2-0	0-0	3-1	2-0	■	3-0		3-0	0-1	1-4	5-0	0-4	1-1	3-0		
Halesowen Town	3-1	0-2	6-0	1-1	3-1	1-0	1-5	2-2	3-1	5-4	2-1	1-1	■	1-2	2-2	1-2	2-0	2-0	1-2	2-0	1-0	0-0
Hastings Town	2-2	0-2	1-0	2-1	0-0	1-0	1-2	1-0	1-0	0-2	2-1	1-2	2-3	■	2-2	2-2	2-2	0-0	2-3	2-2	4-3	0-0
King's Lynn	2-0	2-1	4-2	2-0	2-0	2-2	0-2	0-1	0-4	2-1	5-1	0-2	2-1	1-4	■	2-1	0-1	4-0	1-1	3-2	2-1	0-1
Merthyr Tydfil	3-0	3-2	4-1	0-1	1-2	2-0	2-2	3-1	3-2	1-0	5-0	0-2	1-1	0-0	1-2	■	2-0	5-1	2-3	1-4	1-3	2-0
Newport AFC	3-0	2-0	2-2	0-3	0-0	2-2	1-5	0-1	3-0	0-4	1-3	0-1	0-1	0-2	0-2	3-1	■	0-0	3-1	2-3	3-1	1-1
Nuneaton Boro'	3-0	3-2	0-3	2-1	3-1	3-1	1-0	1-2	3-0	2-0	3-0	1-0	0-2	4-1	2-4	1-1	1-0	■	4-0	4-0	1-1	2-1
Salisbury City	0-1	3-2	2-3	1-1	1-2	1-1	1-2	1-0	0-0	0-4	4-1	1-1	1-2	2-1	2-0	1-3	0-0	1-1	■	0-1	2-1	1-1
Sittingbourne	4-1	1-1	1-0	1-2	0-2	2-1	1-0	3-5	1-3	1-1	1-3	2-0	4-2	2-0	0-2	3-1	3-0	2-2	2-1	■	4-5	0-1
Sudbury Town	2-2	0-1	4-0	0-3	0-2	1-1	1-4	2-0	2-4	2-1	2-0	0-3	4-2	3-0	5-1	1-0	1-1	0-2	0-1	1-3	■	3-2
Worcester City	0-2	3-0	3-0	2-1	2-2	1-1	2-2	2-1	1-0	0-0	4-2	1-2	1-1	3-0	2-1	2-1	1-1	0-1	2-1	0-2	2-1	■

DR. MARTEN'S FOOTBALL LEAGUE
PREMIER DIVISION 1996/97

FINAL LEAGUE TABLE

Gresley Rovers	42	25	10	7	75	40	85
Cheltenham Town	42	21	11	10	76	44	74
Gloucester City	42	21	10	11	81	56	73
Halesowen Town	42	21	10	11	77	54	73
King's Lynn	42	20	8	14	65	61	68
Burton Albion	42	18	12	12	70	53	66
Nuneaton Borough	42	19	9	14	61	52	66
Sittingbourne	42	19	7	16	76	65	64
Merthyr Tydfil	42	17	9	16	69	61	60
Worcester City	42	15	14	13	52	50	59
Atherstone United	42	15	13	14	46	47	58
Salisbury City	42	15	13	14	57	66	58
Sudbury Town	42	16	7	19	72	72	55
Gravesend & Northfleet	42	16	7	19	63	73	55
Dorchester Town	42	14	9	19	62	66	51
Hastings Town	42	12	15	15	49	60	51
Crawley Town	42	13	8	21	49	67	47
Cambridge City	42	11	13	18	57	65	46
Ashford Town	42	9	18	15	53	79	45
Baldock Town	42	11	8	23	52	90	41
Newport AFC	42	9	13	20	40	60	40
Chelmsford City	42	6	14	22	49	70	32

Promoted : — Gresley Rovers

Relegated : — Ashford Town, Baldock Town, Newport AFC and Chelmsford City

F.A. UMBRO TROPHY 1996-97

First Round

Date	Home		Away		Att
18 Jan 97	Gresley Rovers	3	Altrincham	3	927
18 Jan 97	Morecambe	3	Chorley	1	937
18 Jan 97	Workington	2	Bamber Bridge	5	313
18 Jan 97	Colwyn Bay	6	Lancaster City	0	335
18 Jan 97	Gainsborough Trinity	1	Bradford Park Avenue	3	631
18 Jan 97	Emley	2	Boston United	1	504
18 Jan 97	Spennymoor United	0	Bishop Auckland	2	482
18 Jan 97	Northwich Victoria	3	Hednesford Town	1	1109
18 Jan 97	Blyth Spartans	1	Grantham Town	1	667
18 Jan 97	Southport	0	Halesowen Town	0	1005
18 Jan 97	Hyde United	4	Bedworth United	2	512
18 Jan 97	Guiseley	2	Telford United	1	778
18 Jan 97	Kidderminster Harriers	3	Macclesfield Town	0	2815
18 Jan 97	Gateshead	1	Runcorn	2	380
18 Jan 97	Ashton United	5	Moor Green	3	180
18 Jan 97	Stalybridge Celtic	0	Halifax Town	1	973
18 Jan 97	Bath City	1	Stevenage Borough	1	682
18 Jan 97	Slough Town	2	Dorchester Town	2	744
18 Jan 97	Cheltenham Town	1	Dulwich Hamlet	2	703
18 Jan 97	St. Leonards Stamcroft	1	Newport AFC	0	501
18 Jan 97	St. Albans City	2	Weymouth	0	506
18 Jan 97	Rushden & Diamonds	1	Farnborough Town	2	1759
18 Jan 97	Enfield	1	Boreham Wood	3	693
18 Jan 97	Hastings Town	1	Salisbury City	3	389
18 Jan 97	Wokingham Town	0	Woking	1	1575
18 Jan 97	Kettering Town	0	Chelmsford City	1	1528
18 Jan 97	Raunds Town	0	Welling United	1	437
18 Jan 97	Yeovil Town	2	Hayes	2	2458
18 Jan 97	Bromsgrove Rovers	2	Merthyr Tydfil	1	703
18 Jan 97	Yeading	0	Gloucester City	3	245
18 Jan 97	Worcester City	1	Heybridge Swifts	2	724
18 Jan 97	Dover Athletic	0	Dagenham & Redbridge	2	783

First Round Replays

Date	Home		Away			Att
21 Jan 97	Altrincham Town	1	Gresley Rovers	0		573
21 Jan 97	Grantham Town	1	Blyth Spartans	1	(aet)	687
2nd Replay	Grantham Town	3	Blyth Spartans	1	(aet)	874
21 Jan 97	Halesowen Town	0	Southport	2		866
21 Jan 97	Stevenage Borough	6	Bath City	1		1344
21 Jan 97	Dorchester Town	2	Slough Town	2	(aet)	685
2nd Replay	Slough Town	1	Dorchester Town	2		641
21 Jan 97	Hayes	2	Yeovil Town	2	(aet)	607
2nd Replay	Yeovil Town	1	Hayes	2		2310

Second Round

Date	Home		Away		Att
8 Feb 97	Bishop Auckland	3	Northwich Victoria	2	705
8 Feb 97	Grantham Town	0	Heybridge Swifts	1	1223
8 Feb 97	Dagenham & Redbridge	2	Chelmsford City	1	1351
8 Feb 97	St. Albans City	1	Woking	1	2015
8 Feb 97	Gloucester City	3	Halifax Town	0	1118
8 Feb 97	Ashton United	3	Bamber Bridge	1	323

Date	Home		Away			Att
8 Feb 97	Boreham Wood	0	Stevenage Borough	1		1242
8 Feb 97	Bradford Park Avenue	0	Morecambe	1		915
8 Feb 97	Bromsgrove Rovers	1	Hyde United	1		971
8 Feb 97	Welling United	1	Guiseley	1		778
8 Feb 97	Farnborough Town	0	Altrincham	2		691
8 Feb 97	Colwyn Bay	2	Southport	0		928
8 Feb 97	Hayes	1	Runcorn	2		635
8 Feb 97	Kidderminster Harriers	0	Emley	0		2301
8 Feb 97	Salisbury City	1	Dorchester Town	1		727
8 Feb 97	St. Leonards Stamcroft	2	Dulwich Hamlet	1		776

Second Round Replays

Date	Home		Away			Att
11 Feb 97	Woking	3	St. Albans City	1		1907
11 Feb 97	Hyde United	2	Bromsgrove Rovers	2	(aet)	707
2nd Replay (17/2)	Bromsgrove Rovers	0	Hyde United	2		642
11 Feb 97	Guiseley	1	Welling United	0	(aet)	523
11 Feb 97	Emley	1	Kidderminster Karriers	5		1021
11 Feb 97	Dorchester Town	3	Salisbury City	2		713

Third Round

Date	Home		Away			Att
1 Mar 97	Colwyn Bay	2	St. Leonards Stamcroft	2		555
Replay (5/3)	St. Leonards Stamcroft	0	Colwyn Bay	0	(aet)	817
2nd Replay	St. Leonards Stamcroft	1	Colwyn Bay	2		1151
1 Mar 97	Ashton United	2	Hyde United	0		1190
1 Mar 97	Stevenage Borough	1	Guiseley	0		2152
1 Mar 97	Gloucester City	3	Runcorn	1		1129
1 Mar 97	Dorchester Town	2	Woking	3		2942
1 Mar 97	Altrincham	0	Bishop Auckland	1		655
1 Mar 97	Morecambe	0	Dagenham & Redbridge	0		971
Replay	Dagenham & Redbridge	2	Morecambe	1	(aet)	788
1 Mar 97	Heybridge Swifts	3	Kidderminster Harriers	0		1187

Fourth Round

Date	Home		Away			Att
22 Mar 97	Dagenham & Redbridge	1	Ashton United	0		1281
22 Mar 97	Heybridge Swifts	0	Woking	1		2477
22 Mar 97	Bishop Auckland	0	Gloucester City	0		832
Replay (25/3)	Gloucester City	4	Bishop Auckland	3		1829
22 Mar 97	Stevenage Borough	2	Colwyn Bay	0		3082

Semi-Finals (1st leg)

Date	Home		Away			Att
5 Apr 97	Dagenham & Redbridge	0	Gloucester City	0		2077
5 Apr 97	Woking	1	Stevenage Borough	0		3969

Semi-Finals (2nd leg)

Date	Home		Away			Att
12 Apr 97	Gloucester City	2	Dagenham & Redbridge	2	(aet)	4000

Aggregate score 2-2

Date	Home		Away			Att
12 Apr 97	Stevenage Borough	2	Woking	1	(aet)	5163

Aggregate score 2-2

Semi-Final Replays

Date	Home		Away			Att
16 Apr 97	Dagenham & Redbridge	2	Gloucester City	1		2053

At Slough Town

Date	Home		Away			Att
16 Apr 97	Woking	2	Stevenage Borough	1		5810

At Watford FC

FINAL (at Wembley Stadium)

Date	Home		Away			Att
18 May 97	Dagenham & Redbridge	0	Woking	1	(aet)	24376

F.A. CARLSBERG VASE 1996-97

Second Round

Date	Home	Score	Away	Score		Att
23 Nov 96	North Ferriby United	4	Hebburn	0		173
23 Nov 96	Blackpool Wren Rovers	1	South Shields	1	(aet)	136
Replay (26/11)	South Shields	3	Blackpool Wren Rovers	1		225
23 Nov 96	Chester-Le-Street Town	1	Dunston FB	3		114
23 Nov 96	Guisborough Town	2	Prudhoe Town	0		143
23 Nov 96	Whitby Town	1	Billingham Synthonia	0		361
23 Nov 96	Poulton Victoria	3	RTM Newcastle	1		97
23 Nov 96	Formby	0	Tetley Walker	5		77
23 Nov 96	Durham City	2	Easington Colliery	1		175
23 Nov 96	Cammell Laird	0	Bedlington Terriers	2		132
23 Nov 96	West Auckland Town	2	Holker Old Boys	3		40
23 Nov 96	Vauxhall GM	3	Clitheroe	1		102
23 Nov 96	Stewarts & Lloyds	3	Glapwell	2		51
23 Nov 96	Boldmere St. Michaels	3	Belper Town	1		203
23 Nov 96	Dunkirk	0	Cogenhoe United	5		105
23 Nov 96	Oadby Town	3	Arnold Town	1		210
23 Nov 96	Hinckley Athletic	2	Eastwood Hanley	0		
23 Nov 96	Denaby United	2	Newcastle Town	4		188
23 Nov 96	Bridgnorth Town	2	Stapenhill	2	(aet)	97
Replay (27/11)	Stapenhill	1	Bridgnorth Town	2		116
23 Nov 96	Brackley Town	2	Hucknall Town	4		215
23 Nov 96	Gedling Town	2	Barwell	1		74
23 Nov 96	Thackley	0	Louth United	0	(aet)	102
Replay (3/12)	Louth United	2	Thackley	1		71
23 Nov 96	Bury Town	1	Collier Row & Romford	2	(aet)	333
23 Nov 96	Histon	3	Ware	2		101
23 Nov 96	Wivenhoe Town	3	Harlow Town	4		219
23 Nov 96	Woodbridge Town	2	Brentwood	0		148
23 Nov 96	Northwood	3	Chalfont St. Peter	1		171
23 Nov 96	Wembley	0	Spalding United	1		142
23 Nov 96	Swaffham Town	1	Saffron Walden Town	1	(aet)	130
Replay (26/11)	Saffron Walden Town	3	Swaffham Town	0		136
23 Nov 96	Feltham	2	Braintree Town	4	(aet)	78
23 Nov 96	Boston Town	1	Barking	3		139
23 Nov 96	Eynesbury Rovers	1	Concord Rangers	2		130
23 Nov 96	Stamford AFC	2	Lowestoft Town	0		379
23 Nov 96	Diss Town	2	Potton United	1		328
23 Nov 96	Halstead Town	2	Gorleston	1		
23 Nov 96	Tiptree United	0	Southend Manor	3		41
23 Nov 96	Aveley	2	Arlesey Town	2	(aet)	112
Replay (26/11)	Arlesey Town	3	Aveley	2		169
23 Nov 96	Brache Sparta	1	Wisbech Town	3	(aet)	250
23 Nov 96	Ashford Town (Middx.)	0	Burnham	1		83
23 Nov 96	Burgess Hill Town	3	North Leigh	0		254
23 Nov 96	Sheppey United	0	Metropolitan Police	1		56
23 Nov 96	Banstead Athletic	2	Bracknell Town	0		
23 Nov 96	Abingdon United	0	Herne Bay	3		96
23 Nov 96	Reading Town	2	Chatham Town	1		120
23 Nov 96	Whitstable Town	1	Slade Green	0		135

23 Nov 96	Beckenham Town............2	Peacehaven & Telscombe 5		150
23 Nov 96	First Tower United...........4	Hailsham Town 2	(aet)	73
23 Nov 96	Whitehawk......................2	Greenwich Borough......... 3		82
23 Nov 96	Gosport Borough.............0	Saltash United 2		124
23 Nov 96	Chippenham Town..........6	Amesbury Town 0		79
23 Nov 96	Paulton Rovers...............0	Taunton Town.................. 0	(aet)	
Replay (27/11)	Taunton Town 2	Paulton Rovers 1		271
23 Nov 96	Odd Down......................0	Bemerton Heath Harlequins 1		56
23 Nov 96	Falmouth Town................1	Truro City 2		530
23 Nov 96	Christchurch...................0	Mangotsfield United......... 2		175
23 Nov 96	Bridgwater Town 2	Brockenhurst.................... 1		271
23 Nov 96	Wimborne Town 1	Backwell United 2		269

abandoned after 71 minutes due to floodlight failure

Rematch (27/11)	Wimborne Town 5	Backwell United 1		209
26 Nov 96	Haslingden.....................1	Trafford............................ 2		72
27 Nov 96	Brandon United...............0	Brigg Town 3		
27 Nov 96	Seaham Red Star 0	Ossett Albion 4		52
27 Nov 96	Mossley..........................2	Morpeth Town 1		146
26 Nov 96	Nantwich Town................2	St. Andrews 1		100
26 Nov 96	Wick...............................2	Thatcham Town 4		171
27 Nov 96	Tiverton Town..................3	Bideford 0		355
3 Dec 96	Tow Law Town.................5	Murton 2		65
3 Dec 96	Hallam............................1	Sandwell Borough............ 1	(aet)	
Replay (11/12)	Sandwell Borough 0	Hallam 1		72

Third Round

14 Dec 96	Brigg Town 1	Tow Law Town.................. 3		289
14 Dec 96	South Shields...................1	Bedlington Terriers........... 3		182
14 Dec 96	Louth United 2	Whitby Town 4	(aet)	147
14 Dec 96	Dunston FB......................5	Holker Old Boys............... 0		129
14 Dec 96	Tetley Walker....................1	Trafford............................ 0	(aet)	120
14 Dec 96	Hallam.............................1	North Ferriby United 3		122
14 Dec 96	Guisborough Town...........4	Poulton Victoria............... 3		111
(at Whitby Town FC)				
14 Dec 96	Ossett Albion 0	Nantwich Town................. 1		117
14 Dec 96	Vauxhall GM.....................1	Mossley............................ 3		130
14 Dec 96	Gedling Town 0	Durham City..................... 1		116
14 Dec 96	Hucknall Town..................1	Newcastle Town............... 0		493

Abandoned after 33 minutes with the score at 1-0 due to an injury to a match official

Rematch (21/12)	Hucknall Town...........2	Newcastle Town............... 1		367
14 Dec 96	Woodbridge Town 3	Halstead Town 1		224
14 Dec 96	Oadby Town 1	Cogenhoe United............. 3		170
14 Dec 96	Spalding United 1	Bridgnorth Town............... 1	(aet)	259
Replay (21/12)	Bridgnorth Town 1	Spalding United 2		
14 Dec 96	Barking............................1	Saffron Walden Town....... 1	(aet)	127
Replay (17/12)	Saffron Walden Town ...1	Barking 3		
14 Dec 96	Northwood 2	Harlow Town 1	(aet)	177
14 Dec 96	Histon..............................2	Metropolitan Police 1		51
14 Dec 96	Stewarts & Lloyds 0	Southend Manor 1		58
14 Dec 96	Collier Row & Romford 2	Braintree Town................. 2		420

Abandoned after 112 minutes due to a floodlight failure

| **Rematch** | Braintree Town ....1 | Collier Row & Romford .... 1 | (aet) | 312 |

Replay	Collier Row & Romford.... 3	Braintree Town 1		290
14 Dec 96	Wisbech Town 3	Diss Town......................... 0		834
14 Dec 96	Concord Rangers 1	Greenwich Borough 1	(aet)	
Replay (21/12)	Greenwich Borough 1	Concord Rangers............ 3		
14 Dec 96	Arlesey Town 3	Boldmere St. Michaels 0		195
14 Dec 96	Burgess Hill Town............ 0	Bomerton Heath Harlequins 1	(aet)	
14 Dec 96	Bridgwater Town.............. 1	Taunton Town 3		731
14 Dec 96	Mangotsfield United 2	Chippenham Town 1		160
14 Dec 96	Tiverton Town.................. 8	Peacehaven & Telscombe 0		550
14 Dec 96	First Tower United 1	Reading Town 5		169
14 Dec 96	Burnham 1	Whitstable Town.............. 2		158
14 Dec 96	Herne Bay 3	Saltash United................. 0		242
14 Dec 96	Banstead Athletic 3	Truro City......................... 1		
14 Dec 96	Thatcham Town 4	Wimborne Town 1		200
21 Dec 96	Hinckley Athletic.............. 0	Stamford AFC 1		255

Fourth Round

11 Jan 97	Stamford AFC 1	North Ferriby United......... 1	(aet)	338
Replay (21/1)	North Ferriby United...... 1	Stamford AFC 0		318
11 Jan 97	Guisborough Town 4	Tow Law Town.................. 2	(aet)	153
11 Jan 97	Mossley 3	Cogenhoe United............. 2		214
11 Jan 97	Bedlington Terriers 4	Dunston Federation Brewery 1		140
11 Jan 97	Tetley Walker................... 0	Durham City 1		200
11 Jan 97	Hucknall Town 2	Spalding Town.................. 5		645
11 Jan 97	Whitby Town 3	Nantwich Town................. 1		513
11 Jan 97	Barking............................ 1	Woodbridge Town 0		
11 Jan 97	Arlesey Town 2	Herne Bay 3		327
11 Jan 97	Southend Manor.............. 0	Wisbech Town.................. 1		420
11 Jan 97	Mangotsfield United 2	Taunton Town 3		396
11 Jan 97	Thatcham Town 0	Tiverton Town................... 1		568
11 Jan 97	Concord Rangers 0	Whitstable Town.............. 0	(aet)	
Replay (21/1)	Whitstable Town 2	Concord Rangers............. 1	(aet)	305
11 Jan 97	Bemerton Heath Harleq. . 0	Collier Row & Romford..... 1		465
11 Jan 97	Histon 0	Northwood 2		138
11 Jan 97	Reading Town 0	Banstead Athletic............. 2		253

Fifth Round

1 Feb 97	Guisborough Town 2	Wisbech Town.................. 0		585
1 Feb 97	Taunton Town 3	Spalding United................ 0		665
1 Feb 97	North Ferriby United........ 1	Whitstable Town.............. 0		338
1 Feb 97	Durham City 0	Northwood 2		448
1 Feb 97	Mossley 1	Barking............................ 0		413
1 Feb 97	Whitby Town 1	Tiverton Town................... 0		1179
1 Feb 97	Banstead Athletic 2	Herne Bay 0		224
1 Feb 97	Collier Row & Romford.... 2	Bedlington Terriers........... 2	(aet)	506
Replay (8/2)	Bedlington Terriers 2	Collier Row & Romford..... 1		715

Sixth Round

22 Feb 97	Northwood....................... 0	Banstead Athletic............. 1	(aet)	912
22 Feb 97	Guisborough Town 3	Taunton Town 0		845
22 Feb 97	Whitby Town 5	Mossley............................ 1		1543
22 Feb 97	North Ferriby United........ 2	Bedlington Terriers........... 0		707

Semi-Finals (1st leg)
15 Mar 97   Guisborough Town 0   North Ferriby United 2   903
15 Mar 97   Banstead Athletic..............0   Whitby Town 1   1228

Semi-Finals (2nd leg)
22 Mar 97   North Ferriby United 1   Guisborough Town........... 1   1359
North Ferriby Athletic won 3-1 on aggregate
22 Mar 97   Whitby Town.....................1   Banstead Athletic............. 1   2006
Whitby Town won 2-1 on aggregate

FINAL (at Wembley)
10 May 97   North Ferriby United 0   Whitby Town 3   11098

Statistics supplied by –

THE ASSOCIATION OF FOOTBALL STATISTICIANS
P.O. BOX 5828
BASILDON
ESSEX
SS15 5GQ

Telephone (01268) 416020
Fax (01268) 543559

For further information about the AFS please forward a 1st Class Stamp
to the above address together with your own name and address.

SOCCER BOOKS LIMITED
72 ST. PETER'S AVENUE
CLEETHORPES
N.E. LINCOLNSHIRE
DN35 8HU

Phone (01472) 696226
Fax (01472) 698546

Web site: http://www.soccer-books.co.uk
e-mail: info@soccbook.demon.co.uk

BACK NUMBERS

We still have the undermentioned publications available post free at the prices shown. There are very few remaining copies of some of these titles so, please, order any that you require without delay to avoid disappointment.

Year	TITLE	Price	Qty	Order Value	
1992	The Supporters' Guide to Football League Clubs 1993	£4.99			
1992	The Supporters' Guide to Scottish Football 1993	£3.99			
1993	The Supporters' Gde. to Premier & Football League Clubs 1994	£4.99			
1993	The Supporters' Guide to Scottish Football 1994	£4.99			
1993	The Supporters' Guide to Non-League Football 1994	£4.99			
1993	The Supporters' Guide to Welsh Football 1994	£4.99			
1994	The Supporters' Gde. to Premier & Football League Clubs 1995	£4.99			
1994	The Supporters' Guide to Scottish Football 1995	£4.99			
1994	The Supporters' Guide to Non-League Football 1995	£4.99			
1994	The Supporters' Guide to Welsh Football 1995	£4.99			
1995	The Supporters' Gde. to Premier & Football League Clubs 1996	£4.99			
1995	The Supporters' Guide to Scottish Football 1996	£4.99			
1995	The Supporters' Guide to Non-League Football 1996	£4.99			
1995	The Supporters' Guide to Welsh Football 1996	£4.99			
1995	The Supporters' Guide to Football Programmes 1996	£4.99			
1996	The Supp. Guide to Premiership & Football League Clubs 1997	£4.99			
1996	The Supporters' Guide to Scottish Football 1997	£4.99			
1996	The Supporters' Guide to Non-League Football 1997	£4.99			
1996	The Supporters' Guide to Welsh Football 1997	£4.99			
1996	The Supporters' Guide to Irish Football 1997	£4.99			
1996	The Supporters' Guide to Football Programmes 1997	£4.99			

The Supporters' Guide Series

This top-selling series has been published annually since 1982 and contains: – 1996/97 Season's results and tables; Directions; Ground plans; Photos; Phone numbers; Parking information; Admission details; Disabled information and much more.

THE SUPPORTERS' GUIDE TO PREMIER & FOOTBALL LEAGUE CLUBS 1998

The 14th edition featuring all Premiership and Football League clubs.

THE SUPPORTERS' GUIDE TO NON-LEAGUE FOOTBALL 1998

The 6th edition featuring all GM Vauxhall Conference, Unibond Premier, ICIS Premier and Southern Premier clubs.

THE SUPPORTERS' GUIDE TO SCOTTISH FOOTBALL 1998

The 6th edition featuring all Scottish League and Highland League clubs.

THE SUPPORTERS' GUIDE TO WELSH FOOTBALL 1998

The 5th edition featuring all League of Wales, Cymru Alliance & Welsh Football League Clubs + information on the 'Exiles'.

THE SUPPORTERS' GUIDE TO IRISH FOOTBALL 1998

The 2nd edition featuring all Smirnoff Premier & 1st Division Irish League clubs, all FAI Harp Lager National League clubs plus Wilkinson Sword Irish League 'B' Division clubs.

THE SUPPORTERS' GUIDE TO FOOTBALL PROGRAMMES 1998

The 3rd edition featuring information on the Programmes of all Premiership and Football League clubs.

Each of the above priced £4.99 post free – Order from:

Soccer Books Limited (Dept. SBL)
72 St. Peter's Avenue
Cleethorpes
N.E. Lincolnshire
DN35 8HU